THE RUSSIAN MOMENT IN
WORLD HISTORY

THE RUSSIAN MOMENT IN
WORLD HISTORY

✣

Marshall T. Poe

PRINCETON UNIVERSITY PRESS
PRINCETON AND OXFORD

Library of Congress Cataloging-in-Publication Data
Poe, Marshall.
The Russian moment in world history / Marshall T. Poe.
p. cm.
Includes bibliographical references and index.
ISBN 0-691-11612-1 (alk. paper)
1. Russia — History — Philosophy. 2. Soviet Union — History — Philosophy.
3. Russia (Federation) — History — Philosophy. I. Title.

DK49.P64 2003
947'.001 — dc21   2002044717

British Library Cataloging-in-Publication Data is available

This book has been composed in Sabon

Printed on acid-free paper. ∞

www.pupress.princeton.edu

Printed in the United States of America

1 3 5 7 9 10 8 6 4 2

This book is dedicated to

Professor Daniel H. Kaiser and
my teachers at Grinnell College

Thank you all

Contents

❖

MAPS

Preface

MODERN RUSSIA IS IN CRISIS, AND VERY FEW PEOPLE understand why. The most common explanation of Russia's present difficulties — the one most likely to be held by the person on the street — is that Communism didn't work. Just *how* it didn't work is the subject of some debate. *That* it didn't work, and that its failure to function effectively is the root cause of Russia's contemporary problems, is not. There is, of course, more than a little Western triumphalism standing behind this explanation of the modern Russian crisis. Since the Cold War was billed as a battle between competing and mutually exclusive ways of life, it only makes sense that the victors should cast aspersions on the now silenced vanquished. And so they have. But beyond the simple pride of Western analysts, we find ignorance, and especially ignorance of Russia's distant past. Most people, particularly those pundits who take it upon themselves to inform the public about such things, have no real conception of the basic rhythms of Russian history. If they had a good understanding of the Russian past, they certainly wouldn't claim that Communism didn't work, because in many ways it did; nor would they say that Russia's current problems are directly traceable to Communism, because they are not.

In an effort to put Russia's present crisis in its proper context, this book offers a general interpretation of the main course of Russian history within the context of world history. This interpretation might be summarized as follows. Russia is neither European nor Asian in terms of cultural ancestry or historical identity. Rather, Russia is best understood as culturally sui generis and historically distinct. Why? Because Russia was founded in a part of the world where there were no earlier civilizations and in which contemporaneous civilizations were very distant. In other words, Russia was remote in time and space. The country was also quite poor. Early Russia in particular was not a well-endowed place for agriculture (the soil was mediocre at best) or trade (Russia had no open coastline). The fact that Russia was a "start-up" founded hundreds of miles from the rest of civilization in a vast forest did not bother the Russians, that is, until the rise of European power. In the early modern period the well-armed and organized Europeans began to stake claims to various parts of the globe, particularly those areas that they could reach by ship. Uniquely, Russia was able to resist the onslaught of Europe primarily for two reasons. First, Russia was not accessible by sea, so the European powers could not travel easily to the Russian heartland. Second, Russia was ruled by a single-minded autocratic government that enabled it, despite relative poverty, to mount an effective defense against European imperialism. Landlocked and autocratically organized, the Russians fended off the Europeans in the early modern period. Thus began the Russian moment in world history, so called be-

*M// strove to become true
Europeans so did'?
really escape.*

cause the Russians alone among large early modern empires maintained their independence from European hegemony. In so doing they managed to produce the accoutrements of modernity — a bureaucratic state, industry, mass culture, advanced armies — in a non-European way. Again, they were the only empire in the world to do so. The Russian moment ended rather suddenly in 1991, when the Russian ruling class abandoned its centuries-old project to travel its own road.

It is crucial to recognize that there is nothing deterministic in this interpretation. I am not arguing that the present-day Russian crisis was the inevitable result of its history. Far from it. The fact that the Russian ruling class successfully charted its own course for more than four centuries is the result of myriad accidental and contingent events, none of which could have been predicted by even the most insightful sage. But with hindsight we can say with assurance that if any or many of these events had not occurred, then there would have been no Russian *Sonderweg*, no Russian moment in world history, and no modern Russian crisis. The story could easily have been very different, though it was not.

It is equally important to bear in mind that the present interpretation is not one of failure. Rather the opposite. Viewed from the standpoint of the ruling class, the Russian project was a remarkable success. Unlike the elites of other early modern and modern empires, the Russian ruling class held off European power over an extended period of time. Around the globe, one imperial enterprise after another succumbed to European and later Western imperialism. Russia did not, at least not until very recently. Moreover, the Russian elite forged a mechanism for modernization that was distinct from the European path. Where other empires, having been imperialized to one degree or another by the Europeans, joined Europe as economic partners (America) or clients (Africa and Asia), Russia achieved a good measure of economic, technical, and military success independently, or at least largely so. In the end, of course, the Russian road to modernity proved unable to compete with that pursued by the West and its allies. Nonetheless, Russia enjoyed a remarkable run.

Finally, it is crucial to comprehend that this book is intended for a general readership. No particular knowledge of Russian history is necessary to understand its fundamental arguments, though readers who have some familiarity with Russian, European, and world history will perhaps be best prepared to grasp its full meaning. This book does not present any new facts — in the narrow sense — about Russian history. Discoveries of that sort fall squarely into the province of archive-based monographic studies. Instead, this account relies on facts that have been, to a greater or lesser degree, established by monographic research over the past two centuries. Naturally, certain empirical propositions presented here will arouse skepticism among well-informed readers. It could not be otherwise in a wide-ranging exploration such as this, and of course I welcome constructive criticism. Much of the enjoyment of history is found in debate, and I hope that this book fosters its share of it. Neither does this book pretend to be a complete — that is, factually exhaustive — account of Russian history. Completeness is the burden of textbook surveys. Instead, this enterprise, while covering the entire span of Russian history, focuses on several themes crucial to the explanation presented.

It remains to be added that part of the reason I wrote this book was my own dissatisfaction with both the monographic and survey literature on Russian history. To be sure, both serve useful functions: The former is essential for the advancement of historical knowledge (and the advancement of careers in history); the latter is crucial to the process of teaching novices the "who, what, where, and when" of Russian history (and in earning publishers a pretty penny). Rather, my discomfort with most professional writing on Russian history (and history in general) is that it serves only the slightest civic function. Insofar as the citizens of a democracy hold sovereignty and the obligations accompanying it, they need to know — and indeed deserve to know — about their history and the history of others. But my sense is that professional historians (among whom I count myself) are not doing a very good job of informing the citizenry about relevant historical matters in interesting ways. Why? Historical monographs tend to be narrow and inaccessible. Surveys are often bland, uninteresting recitations of facts. What is left? Not very much, at least not very much that would satisfy the professional historian: popular biographies of celebrity political figures, glossy coffee-table books on wars and weapons, sensational historical documentaries on television.

My purpose here is not to criticize professional and popular history but rather to fill what I believe to be an unmet need — namely, to explain in simple terms to lay readers why Russia evolved in the way it did, what significance its evolution held for world history, and what consequences its collapse has for the future of Russia. Readers expecting to find an explanation that rests on and appeals to common sense will, I hope, be satisfied with the result.

THE RUSSIAN MOMENT IN
WORLD HISTORY

1

What Russia Is and What It Is Not

✛

HISTORY IS NOT WRITTEN IN A VACUUM. FOR THE
past several thousand years, men (and more recently women)
have busied themselves with writing factual stories about the
human past. The most popular of them — the Hebrew Bible,
Herodotus' *Histories*, Gibbon's *Decline and Fall of the Roman Empire* — have, by an imperceptible process, seeped into
our consciousness. In this way, the musings of one age about
an earlier period become the mental furniture of a later era.
As the reader of this book will surely realize, we are in possession of a lot of such mental furniture about the Russians.
Medieval monks, Renaissance scribes, Enlightenment belle-
trists, and a discordant chorus of modern scholars, pundits,
and scoundrels have bravely attempted to divine the secrets
of Russians and the history they made. Some of what they
produced is valuable. Much of it, however, is not, for reasons that should be made clear in the course of the following
presentation. It is only appropriate, then, that we begin our
investigation by clearing away this accumulated underbrush

so that we may better see the true visage of Russia and its people.

Of the myriad foolish things that have been said about the Russians, the most foolish is perhaps that they are somehow predisposed to authoritarian government. This notion has a slight grounding in reality but departs rapidly from it with a whole host of ill-considered inferences. There is no ignoring the fact that Russia has been ruled for most of its history by monarchical or oligarchical political regimes. Fantasies about medieval popular councils, Assemblies of the Land, or Boyar Dumas are just that—wishful thinking about what never was and might have been. But to infer from this un-questioned historical regularity that Russians are somehow particularly fit for nondemocratic government is to conveni-ently ignore another unquestioned historical regularity, namely, that popular government is extraordinarily rare in world history, particularly before the twentieth century. It would probably not be an exaggeration to say that demo-cratic government as we understand it is purely and uniquely a product of modern Europe. Before the recent advent of the European-style democratic nation-state (and the weapons that supported and exported it), government basically meant nondemocratic rule. Russia was no different. The exception was western Europe, a point we will have occasion to revisit.

Another misunderstanding concerns the supposed inborn tendency of Russians to expand their borders by war. As with the authoritarian predisposition hypothesis, we have an accepted regularity taken completely out of its proper historical context. That Russia has grown since its birth cannot be seriously doubted, and that Russia has expanded by making war is equally clear. But to claim that Russians are uniquely or particularly imperialistic is to wear historical blinders. The truth of the matter is that nearly all states busy themselves with war-making and expansion, or at least they have until recently. The reasons for this violent propensity are not far to seek. Prior to the later nineteenth century, states were ruled more often than not by warriors; the business of warriors is conquest; and the fruits of conquest are, frequently, territorial gain. It would be ridiculous to expect a prideful, militarized ruling class not to make war. It would be equally preposterous to expect that a warrior elite would yield territory for no reason after conquering it. In short, the Russian elite acted like every other military governing class — it fought other elites for honor and territory. The difference in the Russian case — which commentators almost always miss — is that the Russians usually expanded into territories that were lightly populated by traditional, indigenous peoples. Siberia is the best case in point. The Russians were able to conquer (if not control) all of this vast region in a matter of decades. A look at a map gives the impression that the Russians were master imperialists. But actually they were comparatively poor at the game of conquest. Generally speaking, whenever they fought to advance their western border into heavily populated, well-organized, technically adept Europe, they failed. When they succeeded, their victories proved ephemeral. They could never hold on to their gains.

Often associated with the idea of innate Russian imperialism is innate Russian messianism, and it is equally wrongheaded. The idea of Russian messianism was the brainchild of late-nineteenth-century Russian historical philosophers, men who had read a bit too much Hegel for their own good. Having misunderstood a number of banal sixteenth-century texts concerning *translatio imperii*, they speculated that the Muscovites believed they were the true inheritors of the Roman imperial legacy and its supposed mission to save the known world. Sketchy though it was, the theory of "Moscow, the Third Rome" gained considerable popularity among the chattering classes in Russia and Europe. By the early twentieth century it was quite common to speak of an ingrained Russian messianism. This error was only compounded by the arrival of the Bolsheviks on the scene. Soon after 1917, pundits were explaining the millenarianism of the Soviets with reference to the supposed messianism locked in the Russian soul. As Nikolai Berdiaev put it, the Third Rome became the Third International. Happily, fewer and fewer people took these sort of uninformed rants seriously, particularly as it became clear that the Kremlin's goals— then as now—were rather more temporal than spiritual.

And this brings us to what is perhaps the most widespread misconception about Russia and Russians—that they are European. There is, of course, a very limited sense in which this is true. The Russian heartland is located on the European continent. But as anyone who has ever looked soberly at a map of the world knows, Europe, and every other continent for that matter, is as much a product of human history as it is a given fact about the arrangement of landmasses on the globe. Why, for example, is Europe a continent and India not? They are roughly equal in size, and both are similarly geographically distinct. The answer is plainly that the peoples of India did not decide what should be a

continent and what shouldn't. The peoples of Europe decided this question for the rest of humanity, and they did so
with selfish European values in mind. That Russia ended up
in Europe, therefore, is the result of a relatively arbitrary
historical accident, namely, European dominance and the
force it afforded European geographical conceptions.

Russia, then, is accidentally in Europe. But is it *of* Europe? Russians have wrestled with this question since the
eighteenth century, a time in which being European in a cultural sense had great cachet (particularly for Russia's European rulers such as Catherine the Great, a German). At first
the Russian elite said yes, Russia was European (under Catherine); later they wavered (in the era of Slavophilism); and
still later they proclaimed the question moot (under the in-
ternationalist Bolsheviks). Today they have, in the wake of
the Soviet collapse, begun to revisit this question with confused and troubling results. Europeans, for their part, have
muddied the waters for self-serving reasons. At first they
said that Russia was not European, citing the obvious differences between life in, say, London and Moscow in the seventeenth century (as we see in early European travelers'
accounts). Then in the eighteenth century some of them embraced the Europeanizing projects of Peter the Great and
Catherine the Great and proclaimed that Russia was becoming European (the philosophes, for example). Then, in the
era of the democratic revolutions, "despotic" Russia again
returned to Asia ("scratch a Russian, find a Tatar"). And
finally, a host of starry-eyed socialist fellow-travelers loudly
shouted that Russia was more European (read "advanced")
than even Europe. Today Westerners (as they now call themselves) are unsure of where Russia is culturally, but many of

them still feel that Russia is basically France, just a bit down at the heel.

Nothing could be further from the truth. Anyone who has ever lived in Russia for any length of time knows that the similarities between the West and Russia are painfully superficial, particularly for Russians. It is true that Russia produced brilliant poets and path-breaking scientists and even sent men into space. But the often-heard litany of Russian cultural achievements only serves to amplify the sense of disorientation one feels when standing on Nevsky Prospect, watching a clutch of grandmothers sweep the pitted streets that run past decrepit, cookie-cutter housing complexes. How could a nation that produced such cultural, scientific, and military greatness live in such poverty? This question, which will occupy us for much of this book, is difficult. But a good way to begin addressing it is by admitting that, historically speaking, Russia is not a European country. If it were, then we would anticipate that it would be something like, say, Sweden—a large, northern nation peopled by a prosperous, progressive, democratically minded citizenry. But Russia is not at all like Sweden. It is a large, northern nation with an impoverished, confused, and politically disorganized citizenry.

If Russia is not European in any but an arbitrary geographical sense, then what is it? This query brings us to another misconception of the cartographical variety—that Russia is somehow Asian. Again, we have a tiny kernel of truth: Part of Russia (or rather, the Russian *empire*) is formally located on the Asian landmass. But like Europe, the continent of Asia is a European construct, not a natural fact. This is easily demonstrated. The Ural Mountains are supposed to divide Europe and Asia, but they don't do a very good job of it: They aren't very high and they don't even run the length of the continents they are said to divide. If we accept the puny Urals as a natural continental divide, we might as well say the Appalachian Mountains separate the small continent of Atlantica from the larger continent of North America. This might please the citizenry of the southeastern states, but it hardly makes geographic or historical sense.

So we are forced to admit that Russia is in Asia by historical happenstance. But is it *of* Asia? As they did with the European question, Russians have expended a lot of energy thinking about this issue. Their answer depended largely on the way they felt about being (or not being) European: Catherine and her occidentally minded courtiers liked the idea of being European, so Asia was out; although the Slavophiles didn't like Europe, they were ambivalent about being Asian; a group of Russian exiles in Prague in the 1920s split the difference, claiming that Russia was Eurasian, though they weren't really thinking about geography; and the Soviets dictated that it was a nonissue. Contemporary Russians, reflecting on the failure of Soviet power and the poverty it brought, have taken to saying they are Asians in a distinctly uncomplimentary sense. Europeans have considered the Asian question as well. The earliest travelers to Muscovy sometimes said the Russians were Tatars; Enlightenment opinion distanced Russia from "Tataria"; the nineteenth-century European press liked to call the Russians "Asiatics," again in an unfriendly way; some twentieth-century Western observers noted the similarity between totalitarianism and what they called "oriental despotism." At present (for example, in discussions of NATO enlargement) the Western pundits would have Russia emerge as a regional power, predominately in Asia.

But Russia isn't Asian, because no place is really Asian. The concept itself is a useless artifact of the clumsy, homogenizing European imperial gaze. Europeans proved very adept at making fine distinctions within their own civilizational house — a product, perhaps, of being profoundly and politically multiethnic. Yet they failed completely to capture the diversity of the world they came to dominate. Nowhere is this truer than in Asia. What in the world do Iran, Sri Lanka, and Vietnam have in common? Not much, except they were all uncomfortably lumped into the same bulbous civilizational category. They were all somehow "Asiatic." For its part, Russia — even its geographically eastern parts — shares virtually nothing in common with any of the major Asian cultures, so it could hardly be considered Asian.

If, then, Russia is neither European nor Asian in a cultural sense, what is it? The answer follows necessarily from the observations we have already made: It is *Russian*. As the following presentation will show, the East Slavs who migrated from central Europe to the area that became the Russian heartland were pioneers. They brought with them only the slightest knowledge of the Judeo-Christian or Greco-Roman traditions — the twin bases of Europeanness in a deep-historical sense. Neither did they carry much in the way of general Asian civilization (whatever that might be) or particular Asian civilizations (in fact, they knew nothing of the classical cultures of the Near East, Transoxiana, the subcontinent, or China). Some centuries after their arrival in the north, the East Slavs encountered representatives (to put it neutrally) of all these cultural streams: Scandinavians from the west, Greeks (and their South Slavic emissaries) from the south, and Mongols from the east. But despite these contacts, Russia remained a distant, northern principality, far off the beaten track and therefore far removed from the greater civilizational streams flowing in Europe, the Near East, the Oxus region, and East Asia. It was in this relatively isolated context that Russia and Russianness emerged.

In what follows, we will explore the origins, rise to power, and sudden decline of Russia in an attempt to make plain the meaning of the Russian experience for world history. We will begin by tracing the migration of the Slavs to the north and describing their encounter with a group of Vikings from whom they took their name. Thereafter we will investigate the process by which the Rus' became Russians and emerged as a regional Eurasian (in the strictly geographic sense) power. We will then discuss the fateful turn of the Russians toward Europe and its consequences. One of these consequences, as we will see, was the radical transformation of Russia into an early modern society, one at once similar to and very different from that found in Europe. After this we will track the progress of this new society in the succeeding periods and try to explain why it proved so remarkably resilient. Finally, we will outline the reasons for the collapse of the Russian project in the twentieth century and speculate a bit about the meaning of Russian history in a world-historical context.

2

From Slavs to Rus'

✛

THE MOST SATISFYING STORIES BEGIN AT THE BE-
ginning and end at the ending. They possess the comforting
quality of closure: A man comes to a strange town, things
transpire, and he leaves. As storytellers, historians are aware
of this rhetorical device and therefore write their histories
with what purports to be a beginning, middle, and end.
Alas, the complete history is a conceit, an artifact of the
innate human desire to know the whole story. No history
has a clear jumping-off point, least of all Russian history. As
bothersome as it may be, we just do not know—and probably cannot know—the early history of Russia in any detail.
The available evidence is too poor to establish even the sem-
blance of a beginning, or at least one that could be reasonably defended against the attack of a well-informed skeptic.
But begin we must, and we will do so with the first appearance of the Slavs, their migration to the north, and the
founding of the Rus' enterprise.

✛

The very early history of the Slavs is frustratingly obscure. Archeological, linguistic, and genetic data suggest that they, like nearly all the peoples of western Eurasia, are the descendants of Neolithic farmers who made their way into Europe from the Middle East about 15,000 years ago. Having the benefit of greater intelligence (they were *Homo sapiens sapiens*) and the power afforded by agriculture, these people displaced, assimilated, or exterminated the hunter-gatherers of this landmass, hominids known to us as *Homo erectus* and *Homo sapiens neanderthalensis*. Approximately 10,000 years later, a particularly clever portion of these Neolithic farmers—the so-called Indo-Europeans of the Great Eurasian Steppe—in turn displaced, assimilated, or exterminated their fellows with the aid of another major innovation: domesticated horses and the military superiority they afforded. This brings us to the very edge of recorded history, the onset of the Greco-Roman era. The Greeks, for their part, used still more-advanced technologies—sailing ships, wheeled vehicles, alphabetic writing—to spread their culture through much of the Mediterranean and Black Sea basins. They were succeeded, of course, by the Romans, who built a much more extensive and better-organized empire in Europe, the Middle East, and northern Africa. The Romans were in turn laid low by Turkic Eurasian pastoral nomads from the east—the Huns, or Juan-Juan in Chinese sources. The incursion of these formidable Altaic-speaking warriors set off what romantic German historians liked to call the great *Völkerwanderung*, the diaspora of central and northern European peoples who are the recognizable cultural and genetic ancestors of the large, endogamous groups that would become the western Eurasian nations.

Among the wanderers, we suppose, were the Slavs. Roman documents never mention them, at least not unambiguously. But shortly after the Avar invasion of the mid-first millennium A.D., they appear in both the archeological and written records as a distinct, primitive people living north of the Danube River. The authors of the day called them Veneti, Sclaveni, or Antes, though it remains unclear whether these terms designated all ethnic Slavs, particular tribes of ethnic Slavs, or perhaps (as one author has plausibly suggested) types of Slavic military slaves. How long these Slavs had been in Europe we do not know, but given the absence of references in Roman records, they could not have been in the vicinity very long. Nationalistic Russian historians and their Slavocentric Soviet followers, operating on the dubious principle that ancient origins are superior to modern origins, assiduously probed the early evidence in an attempt to make the Slavs a very ancient people indeed. The Spanish say that one finds in the islands what one brings to the islands. So it was with the Russian chauvinist effort to discover their Slavic ancestors in an era that communicated to our time no evidence that any Slavs existed at all. In short, the Slavs' sudden appearance in the sixth century is a mystery, one not likely to be solved by any technique we currently possess.

One thing, however, is clear: The Slavs were unusually dynamic. Again, using archeological, linguistic, and genetic information, we can see that they managed to do something that the original Neolithic invaders, their successors the Aryan horsemen, and the Greeks and Romans after them failed to accomplish—the spread of agricultural settlements to a distinctly inhospitable region of northeastern Europe. Other western Eurasians (it would probably be unwise to speak of "Europeans" at this early date) probably never seriously attempted to colonize this area for two reasons: Population pressure was low enough that they didn't need it, and from their largely Mediterranean perspective it did not seem worth the effort or even possible. In any case, the only people who dared to attempt to live in the far northeast in prehistoric and ancient times were Uralic-speaking hunter-gatherers, the ancestors of the Finns, among others. Their ancient history is unambiguously etched into the linguistic and genetic record: They do not speak an Indo-European language, and they are only very distantly related to the other western Eurasian peoples in terms of ancestry. It stands to reason, then, that the Uralic-speaking hunter-gatherers were holdouts from the original Neolithic invasion, a group that was never expelled, assimilated, or vanquished by the Aryan migration of 5,000 years ago. How did they manage to survive? The answer is ecological: They invented a way to live in a region that was so harsh that no Mediterranean agriculturalist or Steppe horseman cared about it. They were, therefore, left alone in the great vastness of the frigid north.

Until the sixth century A.D., that is. At that time, some force unknown to us compelled the Slavs to begin migrating from their central European homeland (if that in fact was their homeland) to the northeast. Perhaps the impelling force was population pressure, some rampaging army (the sources mention the bellicose Avars), or the simple operation of the unquiet human spirit. We don't know, and we probably can't ever know. We are aware, however, of the timing, geography, and probable reason for the Slavic conquest on this corner of western Eurasia. In terms of evolutionary time the Slavic advance was astoundingly rapid: By the tenth century at the latest the Slavs had succeeded in displacing the Uralic-speaking peoples from much of the area that would become the Russian heartland. They were able to accomplish this, as we've hinted, by adapting central European agricultural techniques to the north. Agriculture enabled them to produce a greater surplus of food than could the Uralic-speaking tribes, who lived very close to the margin of existence by hunting and gathering. With excess food, the Slavs could afford to maintain classes of people who did not have to gather, hunt, or work the land—traders, artisans, and, most important, warriors. The Uralic-speaking tribes did not have the resources to maintain such classes and thus were left with no alternatives but to assimilate, fight a losing cause, or flee. Genetic evidence suggests they did not assimilate: Finns are not, as we said, closely related by descent to the Slavs. There is no written record suggesting that they fought, nor would we expect to find any—all parties were unlettered. And thus we are left to conclude that the Uralic-speaking tribes simply moved farther north to an even more inhospitable ecological zone, a conclusion buttressed by the fact that they are still there, and only there, today.

Though the Slavs discovered a way to practice agriculture in the north, their lives were hardly secure. Central Russia, despite the common impression, was not a well-endowed area of the globe. Being northerly and inland, growing seasons were made short by the brevity of spring and summer. A peasant planting in the spring could expect to produce only one crop cycle before the first frost in the fall. Moreover, the soil was quite poor, largely due to acidification by the needles of pine trees that cover the region. Of course, the

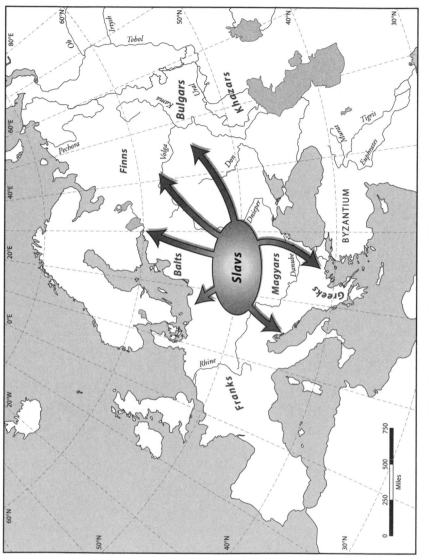

The Slavic Migrations, Sixth–Ninth Centuries

trees themselves were a mixed blessing. On one hand, they had to be cleared in order to make cultivation possible, and pine trees grow back quickly on land left fallow. On the other hand, the forest provided a rich supply of building material (wood), food (game), and medicinal goods (herbs). The Slavs took full advantage of the forest's bounty, but even this resource was not enough to keep them warm and well fed year-round. The difficulty of the northern Eurasian ecology, together with the primitiveness of early Slavic agricultural techniques (predominately scratch plows), probably meant endemic poverty for the great mass of settlers.

Nevertheless, the Slavic agriculturalists succeeded in driving out the hunter-gatherers, settling this unforgiving region, expanding their numbers, and creating the beginnings of a trading network along the many rivers of the region—the Western Dvina, the Volkhov, the Northern Dvina, and, of course, the Dnieper and its tributaries. Their success, however, proved double-edged: The Slavs—or rather their ruling class—certainly grew in wealth and power, but this same wealth and power drew the attention of some rather hostile neighbors, groups who saw the opportunity to poach Slavic trade. These were the Bulgars of the middle Volga, the Khazars of the lower Volga, the Pechenegs and Polovtsy of the Great Steppe, and, most famous, the Vikings of the Baltic Sea. Since only the Vikings succeeded in conquering the Slavs, we should pause to say a few words about them.

By the standards of premodern warrior classes, the Vikings were a rather sophisticated bunch. Of course they have a reputation for being brutes, but this is not in fact the case. Unlike their competitors in northern Eurasia, they did not employ horses as a mode of travel and conquest. Rather they relied on a very specific and highly advanced form of nautical technology — the longship. The longship was remarkable because it was highly durable, relatively light, and, most important, capable of traveling with great efficiency in open seas and tiny rivers. A bit like the airplane, it could go where other modes of transport could not, and it could go there quickly. By a peculiar geographic accident, the longship proved to be perfectly suited for travel around the European peninsula of Eurasia, which was surrounded by reasonably mild seas and crisscrossed with large, slow-flowing rivers. Whereas foot-borne or horse-borne warriors had to trudge across the rough and inhospitable terrain of western Eurasia in search of booty, the Vikings could use the sail to travel around it and oars to move within it. They were the marines of their day.

Sometime near the end of the first millennium A.D., a group of Vikings, probably aided by local Slavic strongmen, took control of the modest riparian trade route from the Baltic to the Black Sea. Just how they accomplished this, we do not know. The earliest Slavic written sources from the region, penned by churchmen, suggest that the local lords were constantly fighting among themselves, not an unlikely thing given human proclivities and the apparent absence of any centralized authority in the region. But the account goes on to suggest that these same disunited Slavic leaders suddenly saw the error in their ways and called the Vikings to rule over them. In light of the fact that this version of events was written well after the Vikings had come to dominate the region, it seems somewhat too comforting to the conquerors to be true. More likely, the Vikings arrived in their longships and made the local mafias offers of "protection" they could not refuse. The Slavic chronicle was produced to explain that they were not conquerors at all but had been invited. In any case, a whole variety of sources from different parts of western Eurasia (Scandinavia, Central Europe, Byzantium) tell us unambiguously that a band of Vikings calling themselves "Rus'" were in charge along the Dnieper in the tenth century.

As a creation of the Vikings, Kievan Rus' (as historians came to call this medieval jurisdiction) shared a common heritage with other early western Eurasian states created or conquered by the Vikings, including regions in England, Ireland, northern and western France, and southern Italy. Indeed the histories of the western and eastern Viking enterprises are quite similar, as the parallel histories of Normandy and Rus' demonstrate. Once the Vikings became sufficiently established in these areas, they gave up their wandering ways and settled down to rule and tax the natives. In essence they traded the hard life of nomadic banditry for the easy life of sedentary banditry. Yet neither the Norman nor the Rus' enterprise existed in a vacuum. Rather the opposite: Both had to deal with the superpowers of the day—Rome and Constantinople. After a bit of violent negotiation, a deal was done: The new Viking kingdoms would be recognized as legitimate if their subjects would accept Christianity. And so it was, though in truth only a tiny portion of the native population had any understanding of the Gospel or, for that matter, of the existence of Rome or Constantinople. Yet there were also local politics to contend with. Being outnumbered by the natives, the Normans and Rus' had to be careful not to push their Frankish and Slavic underlings into rebellion. In any case, they needed native allies, and the best

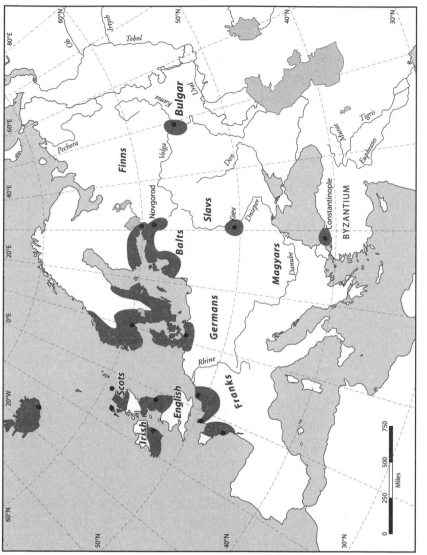

Viking Power and Interests, Ninth–Tenth Centuries

way to get these was by marrying their daughters (a strategy that had other benefits as well). This they did in a process that ended in their complete cultural assimilation by the locals. Within a few generations, neither the Normans nor the Rus' spoke Scandinavian tongues.

Though they were similar in origin and early development, careful examination reveals a number of crucial differences between the Rus' and the other Viking states. Culturally, the western Vikings were successors rather than founders. The Norman kingdom inherited the cultural legacy of older empires, the Roman and Carolingian. The cultural package they found was rich: the Latin language, Roman law, classical letters, the bounty of the Roman Church, not to mention such mundane items as good roads. In stark contrast, the eastern Vikings were pioneers. When the Rus' arrived in the northeast, the Finno-Slavic cultural package they found was functional but comparatively unsophisticated. It contained no hint of the accumulated techniques of classical Greco-Roman culture—no written language, no well-articulated law, no letters, no organized church, and, of course, no roads. The Rus' did receive classical culture via contact with Byzantium, but quite little of it. The written language bequeathed to them by the Greeks had been designed for missions to South Slavic lands, and therefore was difficult for the East Slavic Rus' to understand. "Old Church Slavic" would, in stark contrast to Latin in Europe, remain a liturgical language, and a poorly comprehended one at that. It could never serve as a vehicle for the transmission of classical learning to the Rus'. The Greeks brought some law and letters to the Rus', but evidence suggests that neither were terribly useful or influential. Certainly the greatest contribution made by the Greeks to Rus' culture was Orthodox Christianity. The church integrated Rus' into the sphere of western Eurasian ecclesiastical affairs (via the hierarchy) and transformed Slavic customs (such as polygamy) into Christian ones (monogamy). In the practical arts, the Rus' doubtlessly benefited from Greek knowledge of art, architecture, and various crafts. But the fact of the matter was that neither Greeks nor Romans nor any representatives of a well-articulated classical civilization had ever lived in the region that would soon be Russia, so the technological level of the East Slavs was perforce comparatively primitive.

Economically the western Vikings built their operations on the decayed remnants of older imperial infrastructures, while the eastern Vikings had to start from scratch. In Gaul the Romans had constructed a vast system of fortified towns linked together by well-traveled trade routes. Moreover they had invented devices to make exchange efficient: commercial law, standard weights and measures, uniform money. The Carolingians, and later the Normans, inherited all this, though in rather corrupted form. In the land of the Rus' there was nothing of the sort. The Finns and early Slavs didn't live in cities, nor did they practice much in the way of long-distance trade. They knew next to nothing of commercial law, weights and measures, or money. This is not to say that they were primitive in any essential sense. Far from it. They knew how to live where no Greek or Roman thought possible. But their existence was, as we've seen, marginal: Agricultural practices were crude, the soil was poor, and growing seasons were short. In most years, we imagine, there was very little to go around after everyone had been fed. The lack of an agricultural surplus itself made the development of trading towns and the conduct of trade difficult. Townsmen lived, in the main, on food grown outside the urban walls; the less of it there was, the fewer of them there were. Similarly, high-volume trade is only possible where there are traders and something of value to trade; the Finns and Slavs had neither at their disposal, at least in any quantities.

Militarily the eastern Vikings were at war much more often than their western counterparts. Certainly the Normans and their western brothers were involved in their share of violent scrapes. But in one important respect, western Eurasia across the Elbe River was pacified after the turn of the millennium: The flow of Eurasian nomads—Huns, Avars, and the others—that had flooded central Europe over the preceding centuries ceased. The Magyars were the last to come and settle. After them the post-Roman lands were not invaded from the east until the Russians drove the Napoleonic invaders back to Paris. The story was rather different in Rus'. Here, the nomads continued to arrive and remained very powerful. The early Rus' chronicles are overflowing with stories of Orthodox princes fighting a host of usually nomadic, usually Turkic-speaking enemies. Indeed, hardly a year went by without the Rus' joining some sort of battle with their eastern and southern neighbors. At a time when the western Viking kingdoms were thriving in the renaissance of the High Middle Ages, the Rus' were fighting Steppe warriors for their very lives.

Yet despite these comparative disadvantages, the Rus' were more than reasonably successful. They created or borrowed a functional dynastic political culture based on generational rule: Uncles were succeeded by cousins, and so on.

They built a network of churches and monasteries over their vast territories. They established a modest trading network that brought Arab and Byzantine luxury goods (especially silver) to the north and native products (especially honey, wax, and furs) to the south. And they generally defeated their competitors in the region—the Bulgars, Khazars, Pechenegs, and Polovtsy. Using their trade links to the post-Carolingian lands as well as their clerical links in Byzantium, the Rus' gained in international prestige. They even managed to marry a few of their daughters to German princes.

From the ninth century, at the time of the Viking takeover, to the beginning of the thirteenth century, Rus' progressed from a distant, marginally profitable Viking protection racket to an established western Eurasian empire. The grand prince's writ ran from the Baltic Sea to the edge of the Steppe and from the Vistula River to the upper Volga River. Kiev was a considerable metropolis, and many smaller towns dotted the landscape. International trade flowed along the region's many rivers. The beginnings of high culture were flowering. True, there were problems: The system of generational rule demonstrated a tendency for periodic breakdown, causing in turn a tendency for political fragmentation. By the mid-twelfth century, Rus' was already divided into semiautonomous principalities. Yet it was not some internal mechanism that finally laid the Kievan empire low. Rather, the mortal blow was struck by yet another group of Eurasian pastoral nomads—the Mongols.

The Mongols, like the Vikings before them, have gotten some pretty awful press. In the Rus' chronicles they are godless Hagarites, the orphans of God; in modern times they become "Asiatic" barbarians, the orphans of civilization. The truth is, of course, that the Mongols were the largest, most advanced, and best-led nomadic force ever to cross the Great Steppe. They defeated the most sophisticated empires of Eurasia—the Hsi Hsia, Chin, Kara Khitai, Khwarazim, Abbasid, and Sung. They also subordinated a host of minor, more primitive enterprises, among them the Rus' empire in the northwestern corner of Eurasia. The conquest of the Rus' by the Mongols closes what historians call the Kievan period in Russian history. The skewed nature of this nomenclature should be sufficiently clear to the careful reader by now. We would do better to call this era the Rus' period in East Slavic history.

Terminological quibbles aside, the arrival of the Mongols on the scene had a tremendous impact on the history of the region. Not in the thirteenth century when they appeared, but rather in the nineteenth century—about a half millennium after they had vanished into the trackless plains of Eurasia. It was then that a number of confused historical philosophers decided that the Mongols had diverted "Russia" from its true path of Western development. This interpretation was not based on any evidence found in the sources; instead, it arose from a need to explain the "failure" of Russia, a European nation, to evolve in a European manner. The premise is of course false, but it was far too painful for these Europhilic Russian thinkers to admit. So they looked elsewhere for a scapegoat. The Mongols proved an easy target: They were not very well liked at the time and had in fact invaded Rus'. And so it was that the myth of the Tatar Yoke was born.

In actuality the Mongols had very little general impact on

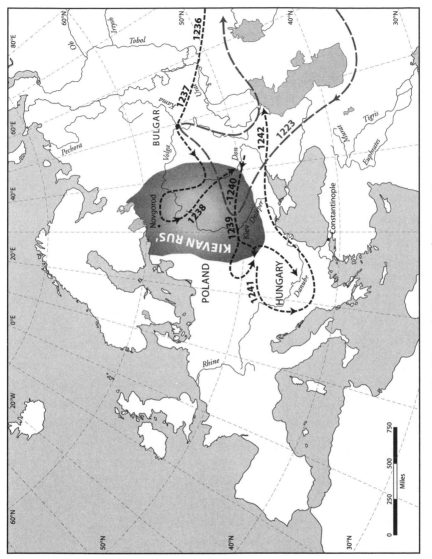

The Mongol Conquest of Kievan Rus'

the course of Rus' history. The Rus' empire was divided *before* the Mongols arrived, so it cannot be said that the nomads destroyed the Kievan enterprise by themselves. Moreover, the Mongols did not care enough about the Rus' to invest the resources necessary to alter the course of the region's evolution. In comparison to China, Transoxiana, India, and Persia, Rus' was a complete backwater. The Mongols did not even bother to settle in the region, preferring the southern climes around the Caspian Sea and the comfortable towns of the ancient central Eurasian empires. Apparently (and the evidence here is hardly clear), the Mongols occasionally sent detachments of tax collectors to Rus'. They gathered revenue from Rus' princes, who were in essence subcontractors collecting rents from native Slavic traders and peasants. This tributary system, like all tributary systems, required a certain amount of coercion (the Mongols destroyed cities to set the right tone) and a certain amount of coordination (the Mongols taught the Rus' the ways of imperial administration for this purpose), but it was hardly the oppressive force described in the Rus' chronicles or nationalistic Russian historiography.

Beyond the fiscal drain of Mongol rule (perhaps offset by increased trade within the Pax Mongolica) and the transmission of coercive and administrative techniques, it is difficult to see how the Mongols could have had any effect on the Rus'. Their cultures were radically different: The Rus' were Slavs, and the Mongols were Altaic. Their religions were different: The Rus' were Christians, and the Mongols practiced shamanism. And their ways of life were at odds: The Rus' were dirt farmers, and the Mongols were pastoral nomads. The only thing the two groups shared was the imperial system, so it is hardly surprising that nearly every remnant of Mongol ways in Russian culture has to do with administration, horses, money, trade, and so on. The Mongols were like absentee landlords — as long as you paid your rent to the collector, you were left alone. And usually the tribute arrived on schedule, thanks to the good offices of the tiny principality of Moscow, to which we now turn our attention.

3
From Rus' to Russia

HISTORIANS HAVE A PROPENSITY FOR MAKING CON-
nections, particularly chronological connections. In fact, the
very mode of explanation that distinguishes history from the
other sciences is chronological: this happened, because that
had happened. Yet we must admit that historians sometimes
read too much into a succession of events and are fooled
into thinking that an earlier event caused a later one. Every
novice historian is trained to avoid the *"post hoc, ergo prop-
ter hoc"* fallacy. But in the case of late medieval Russian
history, this useful warning seems to have been forgotten by
overeager historians striving to make their beloved connections.

For centuries, Russian historians and intellectuals have claimed
that Muscovy was the successor to Kievan Rus'. Like most
overblown, self-serving notions, this proposition contains an
element of truth. The Muscovite tsars were certainly related

by blood to the Rurikid founders of Rus' (so were thousands of other princes, for that matter). Moreover, they certainly claimed to be the imperial successors to the Kievan throne, at least when they found themselves in pompous ceremonies (coronations and such) or in sticky political contexts where such a position would be useful (the annexation of left-bank Ukraine, for example). But all we have to do to dispel the idea of unmitigated succession from Kiev to Moscow is to look at a map of eastern Europe, consider the supposed chronology of succession, and think a bit about what imperial succession might sensibly mean.

Kiev is located in the south on the Dnieper River in the Steppe; Moscow is located far to the north on the Moskva River in the forest. These are radically different places. Of course, empires sometimes move from one locale to another. Oddly, Constantine transported the capital of the Roman empire to a Greek city on the Black Sea. But Russian history has no parallel to Constantine. No Kievan ruler ever decamped to Moscow permanently, nor would he ever have considered doing so — Moscow was too far up the river and too far down the hierarchy of towns for the prideful princes of Kievan Rus' to consider making it their capital. As Kiev declined, such a migration took place, but it was hardly ever billed as a succession. Not only are Kiev and Moscow two very different places, they existed in two very different times: Kiev flourished in the eleventh century, a time in which Moscow was a muddy outpost on a minor river; Moscow rose to glory in the sixteenth century, a time in which Kiev was firmly in Lithuanian hands. The point is that a good three centuries transpired — historians sometimes call this the Appanage Period — in which there was no unified East Slavic empire east of Lithuania, not in Kiev, not in Moscow, not anywhere. Empires do relocate, as the case of Rome demonstrates. But they do not travel through time, disappearing in one period and reappearing in another (except in science fiction, where this is common). Believing Moscow succeeded Kiev is a bit like thinking Aachen succeeded Rome in the era of Charlemagne. It was pleasing for the Muscovite tsars to imagine they were latter-day Kievan grand princes, just as it was pleasing for the the Franks to imagine they were latter-day Roman emperors. But both notions were more comforting for the victors than they were (or are) in accordance with historical reality.

It would be much more sensible to propose that Moscow succeeded Sarai, the seat of a division of the Mongol empire—the Kipchak khanate (or "Golden Horde," as it is called in Russian sources)—on the lower Volga River. The Kipchaks used the Rus' princes as agents in their imperial endeavor. They often played favorites, turning from one prince to another, turning one prince against another, and turning a tidy profit in the process. But the Muscovites, it turned out, were their most dutiful servants. The Kipchaks repeatedly made them chief tax subcontractors (thereby making the Muscovites rich) and made them grand princes (thereby making them powerful). Reading the Muscovite chronicles of the era, one might get the impression that the Kipchaks were ruthless oppressors, bent on martyring Orthodox princes and destroying the Orthodox Church. The truth is otherwise. The Kipchaks patronized the Muscovite princes, in essence entering into a mutually beneficial deal with them: The Kipchaks would acknowledge Muscovite authority in Rus', and the Muscovites would deliver tribute to the Kipchaks. The monks who wrote the chronicles, obviously, could not countenance this duplicity, nor could later historians who perhaps read it between the lines. So it was buried beneath the tale of the Tatar Yoke.

Without a third party to enforce it, no deal is really final. In the case of the Kipchaks and Muscovites, the terms of the deal were subject to constant renegotiation as the balance of power between the two parties changed. Usually the talks were peaceful and the terms were calmly adjusted. Sometimes, however, diplomacy was pursued by other means. This is what happened in 1380 at the Battle of Kulikovo Pole and in 1480 at the Stand on the Ugra River. In the Orthodox Russian chronicles and the nationalistic Russian historiography based on them, these conflicts are depicted as the first and last moments in throwing off the hated Tatar Yoke. Such an interpretation is both self-serving (for the Russians) and highly unlikely (from our point of view). In addition to the fact that there is no primary evidence of any sustained campaign to destroy any Tatar Yoke, such an endeavor would have been manifestly against Muscovite interests. The Kipchaks protected and promoted the Muscovite princes, making them powerful regional lords. It is much more reasonable to suggest that in these two instances the Kipchaks and Muscovites failed to reach an agreement peacefully and decided to raise the stakes. Of course, full-scale war was very expensive and very disruptive. And either side could lose. So the two sides did a lot of posturing, a little fighting, then sat down again to negotiate. In both cases, the Muscovites continued to pay the Tatars tribute.

But Mongol power was definitely waning in the fifteenth century. The charismatic flame of the descendants of Genghis Khan had been largely extinguished; the Golden Horde had broken into khanates; and the ancient states on the southern rim of Eurasia were developing advanced armed forces that used gunpowder—the Ottomans, the Safavids, the Moguls, the Ming. In Rus', it was becoming clear that the Kipchaks could not command the respect they once had. An imperial void was created, one that a series of remarkable Muscovite leaders—Ivan III, Vasilii III, and Ivan IV ("the Terrible")—were only too happy to fill. Ivan III completed the process of subordinating the Rus' principalities to Moscow, thereby uniting the northeast Rus' under one monarch for the first time (not counting the Mongol khan, of course). As in the case of the Mongol invasion, this development was radically misrepresented by nationalistic Russian historians who relied too heavily on stilted Muscovite clerical accounts. Like the Vikings before them, the Muscovites had no desire to be remembered as conquerors of the people they ruled. So they—or rather their monkish publicists—cooked up the story of the Gathering of the Russian Lands. "Gathering," of course, is a rather inappropriate word for the coercion of foreign princes into accepting Muscovite "protection." But the idea was useful, and it remained so in the nineteenth century when all manner of non-Russian territories were being "gathered" and Russified. Hence the Gathering of the Russian Lands took its place alongside the Invitation of the Rus' and the Tatar Yoke in the pantheon of hallowed Russian historical myths.

Flattering fantasies aside, Ivan III, Vasilii III, and Ivan IV used their newfound independence and strength to fill the lacuna left by the dissolving Kipchak khanate. They expanded the kingdom's borders east beyond the Volga River,

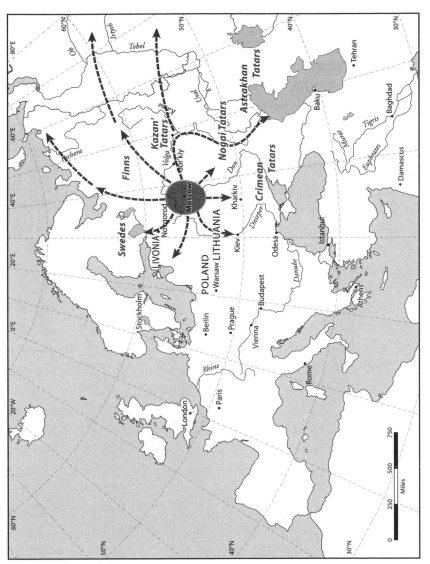

The Rise of Muscovy, Fourteenth–Sixteenth Centuries

south to the Caspian Sea, west to the Dnieper River, and north to the White Sea. In so doing they came to rule peoples who had never been part of Kievan Rus'—Mordvinians, Chuvash, Mari, Samoyeds, Bashkirs, Tatars, Balts, Finns, Germans, Lithuanians, Poles, Cossacks, and Turks, among others. The once homogeneous Muscovite state, located in the uniformly East Slavic Oka-Moskva "mesopotamia," became a huge multiethnic empire. The empire also brought the warrior elite unprecedented wealth in the form of trading cities—Smolensk, Polotsk, Novgorod, Kazan', Astrakhan'. Peasants are hard to tax, and poor peasants without excess grain or money are very hard to tax. Such was the case with the Rus' peasantry: They had little surplus and knew next to nothing of money. Trade, in contrast, is much easier to tax, for three reasons: Goods are usually transported along roads and rivers; they are often brought to centralized markets, usually in towns; and exchange is often conducted in money. All the Muscovites needed to do to levy taxes in the conquered trading towns was to post well-armed officials on the roads and rivers and in the markets. The officers didn't travel to the source of revenue (as in the case of peasant taxation); the revenue traveled to them. Finally, the empire brought the Muscovites into contact with other major states in Eurasia. Prior to the period of expansion, the Muscovites lived in an isolated world dominated by the Tatar khanates (and for this reason sometimes presented themselves as Tatars), the Byzantine sphere of influence (rapidly declining in the fifteenth century and finally eclipsed with the fall of Constantinople), and the powers of eastern Europe (Poland, Lithuania, the Baltic Ger-

man jurisdictions). After the conquests, however, the Muscovites found themselves in a much larger world. To the east
was Ming China, to the south were the Safavids and the
Ottomans, to the west were the kingdoms of central and
western Europe. Commercial, diplomatic, and military relations began with all these states in the sixteenth century.

Of all these places, Europe presented the Muscovites with
the greatest opportunities. It was closest geographically. To
get to China or Persia, the Russians had to cross vast distances and formidable terrain, most of which was in the
hands of predatory pastoral nomads. To get to Turkey, the
Muscovites had to fight their way across the Tatar-con-
trolled Great Steppe, something they were militarily un-
prepared to undertake. But to get to Europe, they merely
had to cross the border with the Baltic German states or
Poland-Lithuania. Europe was closest culturally. The eastern
regions were Islamic, Hindu, Buddhist, Confucian, or ani-
mist. Europeans were Christians, if the wrong kind of Christians from the Russian perspective. The commonality of
Christianity gave the Russians a basis for communication,
despite the fact that the Russians knew neither Latin nor any
other non-Slavic European tongue. Europe was the most
welcoming diplomatically. Beginning in the late fifteenth
century, European powers began to approach Moscow with
proposals of alliance, sometimes against other European
states though more frequently against the Ottomans. Finally,
Europe was the richest, or at least its riches were the closest
to hand. The prospect of expanded trade with Europe was
clearly attractive to the Muscovites (they made deals with
the English, Dutch, and others to facilitate commerce), as

was the possibility of further conquest of European trading cities (victory over the Baltic German cities doubtless whetted their appetites). Slowly, then, Muscovy drifted into the European orbit.

As the Muscovites dealt more with Europe, they shed their Eurasian identity — and here we are of course speaking only of the court elite — and gradually adopted a form of self-presentation that was more in tune with European habits. The most important step in this exercise was the modification of the image of the Russian monarchy. Having long been a part of the Mongol empire, the Muscovites had developed a Steppe style of representation. Ivan III, for example, liked to call himself "khan." This show played well in the East but would not do in Europe. The new Muscovite empire needed a new, European-oriented public face. Since the Muscovites knew almost nothing of Europe, they required help. And they got it, in the person of Sophia Paleologa — niece of the last Byzantine emperor, Renaissance princess (raised and educated in Italy), and the wife of Ivan III. She and her entourage of Italo-Greeks would serve as imperial style consultants to the "rude and barbarous" Muscovites. They had the full support of the Russian Church. While the Mongols were strong, the church had remained reasonably silent as the Muscovite court copied Steppe manners. Once the Mongols had weakened, however, the churchmen grew bold and decided that their onetime overlords were godless heathens. The new official line on the Mongols was reinforced by the fall of Constantinople to the Ottoman Turks in 1453. With the demise of Byzantium, the heads of at least a few Russian clerics were filled with fantasies about Third Romes in Moscow. The new Christian Rome required

a new Christian caesar, not a heathen khan. And so the
Church set about aiding Sophia and her party in their efforts
to Byzantinize the Russian monarchy.

All in all, they did a respectable job of making Ivan III
into a new Constantine and Moscow a new Constantinople,
symbolically at least. A number of cosmetic, European
changes were made: Ivan's Russian title (grand prince) was
supplemented by "tsar" (from the Latin *caesar*) and "autocrat" (from the Greek *autokrator*); his decidedly Russian lin-
eage was crudely traced to Caesar Augustus; his prosaic pal-
ace was rebuilt in Italianate style (with Latin inscriptions!);
and his empire was given a symbol, the double-headed ea-
gle — probably courtesy of the Habsburgs. European envoys
in Moscow noted the difference, puzzling over the meaning
of manifestly Roman imperial regalia in the "Scythian" east.
Muscovy was even given a European name, "Russia" — the
Greek designation.

4

The Challenge of Early Modernity

GENERALLY SPEAKING, CONTEMPORARY HISTORI-
ans do not look favorably on the idea of historical accident.
Like most modern people, they like to think they live in a
world in which the reasons for things are discoverable by
reason. Everything, we say, can be explained by something;
we just have to find out what. As comforting and useful as
this opinion is, it is false. In the course of human events,
sometimes things happen just by accident. There is no way
to explain them other than by the sheer operation of un-
predictable fate. The case of the Muscovites' unhappy and
unlucky confrontation with Europe offers a classic and in-
structive example.

The people who built the Muscovite empire did not, in any
conscious sense, choose the location of their enterprise.
Their ancestors happened to migrate there, it was their part
of the globe by right of succession, and it was where they

did their empire building. Neither did they have anything to do with the earth-shaking events occurring just over their western border. They did not elect to be positioned next to, nor did they play any role in the genesis of, a new kind of human civilization in Europe, one more powerful and dangerous than any to have appeared in world history. Indeed, that this novel form of organization appeared first in Europe was itself something of an accident. Despite herculean efforts, no historian has yet been able to explain convincingly why expansionist, militarily superior, protoindustrial civilization arose first in Europe and not in, say, a very impressive Qing China. But, for whatever reason, fate smiled on the Europeans. Thus, by a cruel turn, the Muscovite elite, having just constructed a new and quite typical premodern empire, found themselves face-to-face with what was gradually becoming the most dynamic historical force in world history. Alas, the Muscovites were not prepared to meet the challenge — not culturally, not economically, not militarily.

Muscovite high culture in the era of Ivan III was an elaboration of the culture of Kievan Rus' (insofar as it was comprehended by the Muscovites), with a slight admixture of Italo-Greek elements. Understandably, it was overwhelmingly religious in character. The Greeks wanted to save the Russians from eternal damnation, not to enlighten them in any worldly sense. Thus they transmitted models of Byzantine Orthodox culture to Rus' and left the entire catalog of Greco-Roman secular learning at home. It is hard to imagine that these religious items were understood in the proper Greek sense by the Rus', for they were profoundly alien artifacts. Nonetheless the Byzantine imports were slowly incorporated into Russian high culture and thereby made Russian

After 1453

themselves. This process of assimilation was aided by the isolation of Muscovy from the civilized world. After the fall of Constantinople, the Russians were almost completely cut off from classical civilization. Before the seventeenth century, we have no evidence that Russians traveled abroad with any regularity and no indication that Europeans (or anyone else) frequently traveled to distant Muscovy. In their isolation the Rus' of the northeast experienced what we might call cultural drift: They adapted the portions of Byzantine culture they possessed to local folkways, transforming them into a new species of culture that we can begin to call properly Russian.

In other historical circumstances, such a cultural complex might not have been inadequate for a thoroughly typical premodern state such as Muscovy. Russianized Orthodoxy provided the Muscovites with a moral code that helped them pacify the violent Eurasian frontier and with a promise of salvation that inspired them to press on through the vale of tears. That the Muscovites were unlettered, uneducated, and technically unsophisticated hardly mattered—this was true of the vast majority of people throughout history. And certainly they knew enough to get by in the harsh climate of the north, which was no mean feat. But as fate would have it, the Muscovites were not living in an ordinary place and time. Immediately to the west of Muscovy a new kind of culture was being born in the Renaissance. In nearly every sphere of human endeavor—politics, religion, philosophy, art, letters—the reconsideration of ancient learning was transforming the intellect of European man. Most important, the Europeans were inventing a way to invent things, very useful and powerful things. By the systematic application of reason to nature, Renaissance scientists, technicians, and craftsmen produced instruments that vastly enhanced the power of humans: armor, guns, ships, navigational instruments, cartographic techniques, and so on. And they learned how to regularly improve and adapt these instruments to changing conditions.

The Russians missed this revolution of the mind and the power that it brought. Muscovite sources from the era contain almost nothing that could reasonably be called Renaissance thought: no philosophy, no science, no political theory, and little literature or poetry. Why? Most basically, the Russians possessed very few classical texts, often couldn't read those they had, and had no schools to teach the languages required (Greek and Latin). Of course the Muscovites could have imported foreign learning. The centrality of Orthodoxy to Russian culture, however, made this impossible. The tsar's court, the church, and the common people demonstrated a marked and religiously based hostility to foreigners and their alien teachings. Europeans were viewed as heretics. Visitors sometimes recorded that Russians fled before them in terror, and Muscovite clerics often could not contain their distain for outlanders, particularly Catholics. Foreign learning was seen as the work of the devil. It was not uncommon for officials and clerics to ban any sort of scientific novelty as inimical to the spirit of true Christianity. Without the textual material of the Renaissance and without the tolerance required to receive it from Europe, the new Muscovite empire remained frozen in a fundamentally medieval cultural context.

The Muscovite economy circa 1500 was larger than that of Kievan Rus' and probably better organized: Markets were expanded and protected, a system of weights and measures was introduced, some money was circulated, and commercial laws were promulgated. Though it remained comparatively unproductive, the peasant-dominated complex was usually sufficient for the needs of the state and its people. The court sent governors out into the provinces to live off in-kind rents and services; imposts and duties of various kinds were collected by officials in towns; and the beginnings of rural tax registers were drafted. Revenue regularly flowed to the center in the form of goods, services, and money. The common people continued to farm the land as they always had, using scratch plows on the acidic soil and supplementing their income by hunting, fishing, and gathering in the forest. There is no evidence of starvation at this time, though one imagines that most peasants were comparatively poor.

Had things remained unchanged, this typical premodern arrangement — a warrior elite living off trading towns and peasants — would not have presented a significant problem. Most territorial states in history were exactly of this type, and many of them lived long and prosperous lives. But due to an unlucky happenstance, economic conditions immediately to the west of Muscovy were changing dramatically. As the Renaissance was transforming European culture, a great commercial revolution was sweeping the continent. Agricultural yields improved as new techniques and crops were introduced; large manufacturing centers developed in growing cities; the volume of trade and the extent of commercial networks expanded; silver money flooded in from the New World; and banking centers and new commercial instruments evolved in various European capitals. This economic transformation amounted to what some economists have called the "European Miracle," signaling both the unlikelihood of the event and its world-historical impact. Whether it deserves this billing or not, one thing is certain: The Europeans had evolved a kind of economy that proved more productive than any in history.

Muscovy was untouched by this economic upsurge. In gross structural terms, the Muscovite economy remained fundamentally unchanged from 1400 to 1650. Its huge peasantry was poor, its merchant class was anemic, it hosted no mining or industry to speak of, and it lacked any but the most basic commercial instruments. Why? In the first instance, Muscovite peasants—who farmed poor soil with primitive techniques—had too little to spare to support an entrepreneurial merchant class, the motor of early modern economic development in Europe. The peasants' excess income (when there was any at all) was invested in more children—a rational strategy for an environment in which labor was in short supply and land was abundant. The court and church were too poor to support more than a few traders and craftsmen. The Muscovites might have relied on foreign traders and techniques, but, as in the case of cultural imports, these were seen as spiritually dangerous. This religiously grounded prejudice impeded the transfer of capital and technology that might have stimulated economic growth. Without sufficient demand to support an entrepreneurial class and unwilling to permit large numbers of foreign traders into Russia, the Muscovite economy remained medieval in nature.

Muscovy's greatest achievements in the age of Ivan III were military. Ivan managed to build a large and formidable cavalry, probably modeled on Tatar forces. Its men were highly trained horsemen armed with excellent composite bows of eastern manufacture. He deployed this army to defeat or subordinate Muscovy's traditional opponents (and sometime allies) on the Steppe—the Tatar khanates. The borders of his realm were pushed to the Volga and well south of Moscow. He subdued the city-states of Novgorod and Pskov in the north and attacked the Baltic Germans and the Lithuanians in the west, though he had limited success on this front. At the end of his reign, Ivan ruled a well-armed and fortified empire unmatched in size in western Eurasia. His potential enemies—Lithuania, Sweden, the Baltic Germans, the Cossacks, and the Tatars—posed no real threat.

Had the strategic situation remained unchanged, it seems reasonable to suggest that Muscovy would have been strong and secure for many decades. Unfortunately, however, Muscovy's geopolitical circumstances were radically altered by a revolution in arms occurring on Muscovy's western horizon. During the Renaissance, gunpowder and drill transformed the European way of war: Ill-disciplined hordes of mounted knights were replaced by a mix of forces including disciplined cavalry and infantry armed with firearms, pikes, and field guns. European armies were bigger, better trained, better organized, and more lethal than any military forces in history. More often than not, whenever the European new model armies encountered traditional forces—warriors with cold arms, perhaps on horseback—they obliterated them. For those Eurasian states and empires that were not immediately subdued, the message was clear: Adopt the European-style army or suffer the consequences.

The Muscovites were slow to react to this new challenge.

Over the course of the sixteenth century they imported and deployed gunpowder charges (used by sappers), cannon, and firearms. Yet they continued to rely heavily on the cavalry arm and never really put the gunpowder weapons to good use. As a result, they were repeatedly mauled by European — and especially Swedish — forces in the later sixteenth and seventeenth centuries. Why? Most basically, the Muscovites did not know how to make gunpowder weapons or train troops to use them. This knowledge could be gained only from Europeans, but it was both very expensive and deemed by clerical authorities to be spiritually harmful. In the end the Muscovites were compelled to hire foreign mercenaries, but they could neither afford nor tolerate sufficient numbers of them to defeat the Livonians, Poles, and Swedes. In order to supplement their small gunpowder forces, therefore, the Muscovites continued to deploy medieval cavalry in the west, usually with poor results.

As we have seen, Europe was attractive to the Muscovites for many reasons — it was nearby, Christian, welcoming, and rich. But it was also incredibly dangerous. The Muscovite leaders who opted to engage Europe could not have known of this threat. In fact, no one could have, for even the Europeans themselves did not realize that they possessed cultural, economic, and military tools that would, with time and effort, enable them to subdue most of the globe. With the aid of hindsight, we can see what they could not: The premodern Russians had entered the breach to early modernity, and they were not prepared.

5

The Origins of the Russian Moment

IT IS DIFFICULT TO JUDGE THE METTLE OF A PEO-
ple until they are challenged. The routines of daily existence
allow most of us to sleepwalk through time without troubling our innermost reserves of physical, intellectual, and
moral courage. The extent of our character remains hidden
under the blanket of normality. But some are not allowed
the privilege of self-ignorance. They are challenged and must
react, and in the process they come to know the measure of
their abilities. In the early modern period, as we have just
seen, the Russians were called to the test. We will presently
see how they fared, and readers can judge for themselves the
mettle of these people.

The Muscovites had built a premodern kingdom at precisely
the time when premodern kingdoms were becoming obsolete. They were hardly alone: The Incas, Aztecs, Ottomans,
Safavids, Moguls, and Qing—typical premodern empires

all — found themselves in similar strategic positions vis-à-vis ascendant European power or modernizing competitors. Over the course of the sixteenth, seventeenth, and eighteenth centuries all of these empires — *save the Muscovites* — fell under the hegemony of Europe or, at the very least, were brought low by non-European power (the Muscovites included). The Incas and the Aztecs were crushed by the Spaniards in the sixteenth century (and then were wiped out by the diseases the latter carried); Afghan forces brought an end to the Safavid Iranian empire in 1722, and the Qajar empire that succeeded it came to be dominated by the British and Russians; the British East India Company held sway over the Mogul empire by the end of the eighteenth century, and British control in most of the subcontinent was complete by the mid-nineteenth; the Qing conquered the Ming, and then several European powers united to begin dismantling the Qing empire in the mid-nineteenth century; the Ottoman empire became the impotent "Sick Man of Europe" in the nineteenth century.

Russia was the only extra-European empire to remain a powerful, independent world-historical state throughout the early modern period. To be sure, Russian power waxed and waned from the sixteenth to nineteenth centuries. Twice — during the Time of Troubles in the early seventeenth century and the Napoleonic invasions in the early nineteenth century — Moscow was occupied by European forces. But the fact remains that the Russians faced far more powerful European armies far more often than any other extra-European state and managed to survive nonetheless. How did they accomplish this remarkable feat?

The most basic reason is geographic. If we look carefully

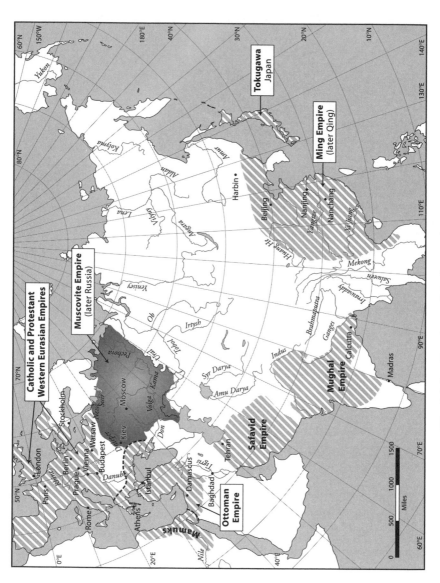

The Major Empires of Early Modern Eurasia

at the spatial pattern of early modern imperialism, two regularities appear. First, if an empire was located immediately adjacent to a powerful competitor, then its chances of survival declined. This was the case with the Ming and the Ottomans, both of whom were brought to heel by empires in very close proximity to their capitals—the Qing in the former instance and a combination of western Eurasian powers in the latter instance. Second, those empires with open coastlines suffered a distinct strategic disadvantage insofar as hostile powers could access them by sea. This was the case with the Incas, Aztecs, Iranians, Moguls, and Qing, all of whom were to one degree or another the victims of seaborne European imperialists in the sixteenth through nineteenth centuries.

Seen in this perspective, the Muscovites and later Russians were perfectly positioned to survive the predation of this era. After the conquest of the khanates of Kazan' and Astrakhan' in the mid-sixteenth century, the Muscovites had virtually no serious competitors in the part of northern Eurrasia they occupied. Moscow was protected from the Swedes, Lithuanians, Poles, and Ottomans by hundreds of miles of formidable terrain. This did not stop these groups from invading the Russian heartland on several occasions, it is true, but it did prevent them from penetrating it easily or, if they managed a deep thrust, from holding it for any period of time. The Poles took Moscow, but they could not rule Russia. No European power farther to the west even attempted to invade Russia before Napoleon, and he simply repeated the sad experience of the Poles. Muscovy proper was virtually landlocked before the sixteenth century, when it began a modest commerce through one or another Baltic ports (which proved difficult to hold) and Archangel on the White Sea (which was frozen for most of the year). This being the case, there could be no question of ship-borne invasion by any European power before the eighteenth century. With the building of Saint Petersburg and the capture of the northern littoral of the Black Sea, Russia gained continuous access to the sea, and Europe gained seaborne access to Russia. But the water gate was, comparatively speaking, very narrow. Only once, during the Crimean War in the mid-nineteenth century, did the Europeans seriously attempt to invade Russia by sea. The Crimean campaign was in many ways a remarkable achievement, but it hardly proved a lasting success.

Russia, then, was protected by an accident of geography from the storm of early modern imperialism that swept over the world. But geography alone does not explain the survival of Russia. Russia was inaccessible, but only relatively so. As a simple glance at a map of western Eurasia will demonstrate, Russia shares a long open border with what we now call Eastern Europe. In strictly spatial terms, Russia was in fact closer to the most hostile powers of the period — those in western Europe — than any other early modern empire. Not surprisingly, it was invaded more often and with more force than any other early modern empire. Thus, even accounting for the difficulty presented by Moscow's strategic isolation, we have to imagine that the Muscovites mounted an impressive defense. And so they did, with the aid of an efficient form of political organization: autocracy.

Autocracy is a species of monarchy. While monarchy is the rule of one, autocracy is the unconditional rule of one. Of course, there is no such thing as the unconditional rule of

one (any more than there is the rule of one); there are always conditions (whatever they may be called), and even
absolute rulers never rule alone but rather in cooperation
with other elites. This fact has led some historians to speculate that all autocracies are, in reality, limited oligarchies.
Some may be, but not the Muscovite one. In the Russian
case, the autocrat was formally unlimited by any but divine
law. Certainly the autocrat's hand was stayed by custom, but
this is hardly enforceable law. Moreover, the supposed oli-
garchs who putatively shared power with the tsar were in
fact men who called themselves slaves and behaved — or
were expected to behave — as such. This is not to say that
they were treated badly; far from it. In the normal course of
events, the tsar's elite servitors enjoyed privileges, power,
and wealth that were utterly unimaginable to the common
peasant. But they were, nonetheless, under the strict control
of their master, bound to do his bidding as long as he did
not transgress God's law.

Living in a democratic culture that prizes personal freedom, Westerners have difficulty understanding how such a
state of affairs could exist. How, we wonder, could men
willingly bind themselves into political slavery? Isn't such an
act somehow contrary to human nature? Quite the opposite.
It is very natural, given the evolutionary history of humans.
Subordination to the strong is a completely logical and functional survival strategy for the weak, so logical and functional that it has been built into the fabric of humankind.
No society in history has been without hierarchy, nor could
any stable sodality be possible without it. The Muscovite
political system is nothing more or less than a particular ad-
aptation of this innate human organizational tendency to a

particular set of historical and ecological circumstances. Autocracy fit historically because the Rus' had been taught by the Greeks that it was the only possible form of Christian government. As God ruled in heaven, so the autocrat ruled on earth. The stories of the Bible—practically the only form of political philosophy available in Rus'—confirmed this dictum; wasn't King David an absolute, divinely sanctioned ruler? Autocracy fit ecologically because of the extreme insecurity of life in Rus'. The northern environment was very dangerous: A simple mistake or accident could result in freezing, starving, or violent death. Given this unpredictability, there was no room for rugged independence. Everyone from the lowest plowman to the highest courtier needed a protector as insurance against the environmental and human elements. The more powerful one's protector, the higher one's status. It is no wonder, then, that only elite military servitors in Muscovy were permitted to called themselves slaves of the tsar.

Autocracy proved important because it provided the warrior elite with what military planners call unity of command. The tsar and his advisors commanded, the ruling class (the "slaves" just mentioned) executed, and the mass of unorganized peasants complied or suffered the consequences. Comparison helps explain this cardinal organizational advantage. In most early modern states, power was divided among several groups. These groups could be religious (the church), economic (incorporated towns), or political (estates). Often their interests were represented on the national level in representative institutions of feudal origin. The Muscovite situation was much simpler. Recall that Rus' was a pioneer state. The eastern Vikings encountered none of the

social complexity that their western brothers did, for the obvious reason that there was no tradition of social complexity
in the far north. Rus' society was remarkably homogeneous
by Eurasian standards: There was the tiny warrior class, a
few townsmen, and a mass of peasants, hunters, and gath-
erers. And so Rus' remained, by and large, into Muscovite
times. The warrior class, organized autocratically, had no
serious competitors in society; the church, insofar as it legit-
imized autocracy and the policies it undertook, was closely
allied with the state. There were no powerful commercial
interests to speak of in Russia, though there was a small
trading class. And Russia had no legal estates, though Muscovite society was divided into a number of status groups. In
the mid-sixteenth century, the tsar created a representative
institution of sorts, the so-called Assembly of the Land. It
did not, however, represent the interests of society before the
ruling class. Rather, the assembly provided a mechanism by
which the warrior elite could consult with its foot soldiers. It
was most often a staff meeting, not a parliament.

With the advantage of unity of command, autocracy enabled the warrior class to undertake reforms that more complicated and fragile political systems could not safely attempt. Consider the dilemma faced by any reforming leader
in a complex political system: Change is necessary, but it
will often run counter to the interests of various organized
groups. If the groups resist with enough force, the leader
may be toppled or the whole system descend into chaos. The
Muscovite autocrat was not regularly confronted by this dilemma, for there were no organized interests in his realm, or
rather there were no organized interests that he did not create and maintain. In an autocracy the battle of interests is

muted to the extent that it may appear that there are no politics at all. This is what many visiting Europeans said when observing the Muscovite polity. They saw no politics in the familiar sense of organized conflict; all they observed was servile obedience. Of course Russian autocracy had its own form of politics — elite men and their families struggling for positions at court. But the principle of autocratic rule was never questioned in these conflicts.

The warrior class, then, used the mobilizational means provided by autocracy to enact radical reforms to compensate for Russia's deficiencies vis-à-vis the ascendant European powers. These reforms can conveniently be divided into three categories: cultural, economic, and military.

The Muscovite elite needed European culture. Russian learning, technology, and weaponry were all acknowledged by the Russians themselves to be inferior. The Orthodox warrior elite, however, demonstrated a distinct distaste for everything European of a nontechnical nature. The Europeans, after all, had fallen from God's grace, or so the Orthodox clerics said. Thus the Muscovites needed to be extremely selective about the things they imported and to make sure that the contagion of European influence did not escape into the Russian body politic. The warrior class accomplished this selective assimilation, first of all, by closing the borders: Foreigners were not allowed to enter Muscovy, and Russians were not permitted to leave the country without the express permission of the tsar. Naturally the elite was not entirely successful in quarantining the Orthodox population, but its intent is significant. Second, the elite recruited a few foreign scholars — Greek monks, German doctors, Ukrainian humanists — but only for very limited purposes. All the foreign experts were under the direct jurisdiction of the court and generally lived under state supervision in Moscow, where they often complained of being held like prisoners.

The warrior class took even more drastic economic measures to protect itself. European and Ottoman military pressure compelled the Muscovites to increase the number and alter the types of forces they fielded. The elite, alas, could not raise sufficient cash for this purpose from the tiny trading class or the poor peasantry. The only asset the ruling class possessed that might be traded for military service was land. So in the sixteenth century the court nationalized a major portion of all productive land and distributed it in parcels to cavalrymen as conditional tenures. This reform produced the required army, but it also froze the land market. Land nationalization did not, however, produce a permanent solution. The free peasants who worked the estates of warriors were quite mobile. They would often seek better working conditions with new masters or strike out for some new region. Peasant flight left the conditional estates without sufficient labor, the estate holders without sufficient income, and the court without a sufficient army. So, in the early seventeenth century, the ruling class nationalized a major portion of all peasant labor and bound it to the land. This measure ensured that the cavalry army would live on, but it also froze the labor market. It remains to be added that the warrior class imposed a virtual monopoly on foreign trade and certain domestic items (especially liquor, which proved to be a major and steady source of government revenue). These monopolies increased state incomes, but they interfered with the operation of markets.

The ruling class reformed the Muscovite army as well. The court knew by hard experience that European gunpowder armies were superior to their cavalry hordes. Obviously some means had to be found to import European military techniques. But as we've seen, the Orthodox Muscovites were resistant to European culture, and they did not possess the economic resources to buy and retain a modern army. Their solution to this problem was ingenious. First, the warrior class continued to deploy the cavalry—supported by conditional tenures and serf labor—wherever possible. This measure reduced defense expenditures and provided security in the Great Steppe, where old-style Russian forces were still competitive. Second, they limited contact with foreigners by hiring as few European officers as possible and by importing (instead of manufacturing) most firearms. This measure provided them with the expertise and weapons needed to begin organizing a Russian gunpowder army. Finally, the elite concentrated its military energies on the capture of peripheral trading towns, particularly the rich European cities of Lithuania and the Baltic littoral. The captured borderlands would serve double duty: They would produce the cash necessary to continue military reform, and they would function as an imperial buffer zone between Moscow and hostile powers.

For any student of modern history, the three sets of measures undertaken by the Muscovites in defense of their enterprise do not, on their face, seem terribly unusual. After all, most premodern states sought to control their borders, regulate the use of land and labor, and modernize their armies by importing more effective techniques and technologies. And many modern states—notably Nazi Germany, Stalinist Russia, and Maoist China—have prosecuted reform programs far more radical than anything imagined by the Muscovites, or so it would seem. But it would be a mistake to downplay the world-historical significance of Muscovite social engineering or to call it in any way typical of its place and time. The reforms were anything but ordinary. In most western Eurasian states, borders were relatively uncontrolled, the factors of production were relatively freely exchanged, and military reforms were undertaken in an organic fashion. Only in Muscovy were the borders closed, universal or near universal state ownership of land and labor imposed, and forced military reform undertaken. We can find bits and pieces of this program in various parts of the early modern world. But Muscovy was unique in pursuing, and pursuing successfully, the entire suite of radical reforms.

And here we find the answer to our question concerning the paradoxical survival of Russia. Using the mobilizational tools provided by autocracy, the Muscovite warrior class was able and willing to do what the Incas, Aztecs, Ottomans, Safavids, Moguls, and Qing could or would not do— transform their societies in order to protect their interests. As we will presently see, the results of this reform effort led to the emergence of a kind of social organization that had never before been seen on the globe, one whose entire history is inextricably linked to Russia and its struggle with Europe. This is the origin of the Russian moment.

6

The Progress of the Russian Moment

SOME HAVE ARGUED THAT THE TRUE SUBJECT OF
history is change. If one thing happens and another does not
follow, then there is no history at all, no story to be told.
While intuitive, this view of history is unduly narrow. For
sometimes the story is that nothing changed, particularly
when all around the stationary point other things were mu-
tating. Russian history in the post-Muscovite period offers
an excellent case in point.

The Russian moment in world history began when the Muscovite elite created the first sustainable society capable of
resisting the challenge of Europe. Here the Russians succeeded where others had failed (or would fail). We have already laid out in sufficient detail the course of the reforms
that molded this society in the sixteenth and seventeenth
centuries. We will now investigate their results.

The most significant consequence of the Muscovite reforms was to make Russia *early modern*. What is early modernity, and what distinguishes it from premodernity and modernity? The answer is complicated, of course, but we can sensibly limit our definition of early modernity to a combination of four distinctive features: a complex administration, a semipublic sphere, the protoindustrial production of goods, and a gunpowder military. By this definition, almost all the major states of western Europe were early modern by the early sixteenth century. So were the Ottoman, Mogul, and Qing empires, for that matter. As we have indicated, Muscovy in this era was not. In the fifteenth century, Rus' was administered by a tiny court and its scriptorium; it had no distinct public discourse; its economy was overwhelmingly agrarian; and its army equipped with cold steel.

By the early eighteenth century, however, Russia was definitely early modern in our narrow sense. The country was administered by a semibureaucratic organization under the direct control of the crown. In the *prikaz* system, officers ran offices with discrete competencies according to acknowledged written rules. True, they were poorly organized, venal, and corrupt. But even the *prikazy* were a major advance over the casual household administration that had come before, at least in terms of the organization of the court's affairs. At the same time, something approximating a public sphere was forming at the Russian court and in major urban areas. Salons, assemblies, clubs, and a tiny press all made their first appearance in Peter the Great's day. Highborn subjects began to read and to discuss what they had read. To be sure, the crown carefully monitored and limited the flow of ideas, but nonetheless the seed of a truly public discourse was present. By late Muscovite times, the production of goods — and particularly arms — was being organized in new, more efficient ways. In the Petrine era, Russians built their first primitive factories to produce basic industrial goods on a large scale — metals, ceramics, explosives, and the like. Finally, the Russian army of the later seventeenth and eighteenth centuries made full use of gunpowder weapons, drill, and unit-based organization. It fought and defeated advanced European forces, such as those fielded by the Swedes in the Great Northern War.

Though they arrived at roughly the same infrastructural place, the origins of early modernity in Europe and Russia were manifestly different. Historians have worked for decades trying to determine when and how the Europeans set out on the road to modern existence. No compelling answer has been forthcoming because the European road has no salient, recognizable beginning. The classical legacy, the barbarian invasions, the renaissance of the High Middle Ages, the Renaissance itself, the limitation of monarchical power, the growth of liberal thought, the commercial revolution, the military revolution, exploration and imperial conquest — all contributed in one way or another to the evolution of early modernity in Europe. *Evolution* is the key word here, for while early modernity in Europe was definitely created by human hands, it had no single creator. The origins of early modernity in Russia were both later than in Europe and much more distinct. They are to be found exactly in Russia's initial response to the threat of Europe, in the reforms of Ivan IV, Aleksei Mikhailovich, Peter the Great, and so on. In contrast to the imperceptible and untraceable evolution of early modernity in Europe, early modernity in

Russia was initiated by these men at that time in a conscious defensive effort.

The Russians also used very different means to build early modern institutions than did the Europeans. The reason has to do primarily with the availability of modernizing resources in their respective societies: Europe had them; Russia really did not. Since Montesquieu first discussed the role of intermediary bodies in monarchies, such entities — organized estates, incorporated towns, clerical organizations, guilds, local parliaments, and the like — have been viewed primarily as breaks on unbridled monarchy. And so they were, as the Muscovite case suggests. But it is important to understand that intermediary bodies were also sources of social power. They could do things that, in the course of modernization, became necessary to the state. Therefore, the degree to which they were available in society determined to a significant extent the strategy monarchs would employ in modernizing. To put this choice in the starkest terms, a monarch could buy them if they were available, or a monarch could build them if they were not. We see this theoretical difference actualized in the cases of early modern Europe and Muscovy. European monarchs had to do comparatively little state-sponsored social engineering in their state-building efforts. Rather, they simply appropriated resources available in their respective societies. In contrast, the Russians, bereft of similar resources, were forced to create them in society by means of social engineering. We can see the difference between these two patterns of state-building in the development of complex administration, the public sphere, protoindustrial production, and the gunpowder army.

In their effort to develop complex administration, European monarchs were able to copy existing patterns of organization (for example, from the church), hire skilled administrators, and, when necessary, employ members of the intermediary bodies to do their bidding. All this came at a political price, of course. Buying an administration was expensive, and taxes had to be raised. Raising taxes, however, brought forth a demand for a political voice from servants and taxpayers. Hence monarchies became limited. In Muscovy, the autocratic state built the first complex administration *ab novo*, for there were no administrative resources in Muscovite society. The people who paid for this effort — traders and peasants — were so disorganized and under the thumb of the court that they could hardly demand any sort of representation.

Because European society was complex, the public sphere evolved within a multipolar political context: The court, the nobility, the towns, the church, and other agents each had independent power and an independent voice. Using the representation afforded them by limited monarchy, these organized groups lobbied the crown in public forums regarding issues of interest to them. In Muscovy, the public sphere was created within a unipolar political context: Only the tsar and the church speaking in one voice were permitted public expression of any kind. Therefore, when the Muscovite and Imperial courts deemed it necessary to promote discussion, they carefully prescribed the means, mode, and overall rules. The Boyar Duma, the Assemblies of the Land, and the Petrine Senate all fit this model of state-created and state-oriented public discourse.

Western protoindustrial ventures were for the most part

created by private initiative within the context of restricted, though still in some measure free, markets. The crown created a legal and fiscal environment that allowed organized, capitalized interests in society to provision private and public goods via markets. In Muscovy and early Imperial Russia, the state alone had the authority and power to organize new forms of production. There could be no question of markets, for Russian society at the time contained neither producers nor consumers of industrial goods. The state simply made what it needed for itself. In the seventeenth and eighteenth centuries there was hardly a mine, manufactory, or foundry that was not created by the tsar's initiative. The very few exceptions — the enterprise of the Stroganov family in the Urals — only prove the rule.

In Europe the development of large, well-organized gunpowder armies was stimulated by the operation of what was basically a lively market in military units. Throughout the early modern period, captains (military enterprisers) raised, trained, and armed troops for this market. Consumers (kings, princes, towns, and parliaments) paid handsomely for top-of-the-line gunpowder units, and this stimulated further innovation in arms and tactics. The cases of the famous Swiss and Hessian mercenaries are perhaps the best-known examples of this type of enterprise. In early modern Russia, only the state could raise, train, and arm troops, because only the state had the resources to accomplish this feat. There were no military entrepreneurs other than those of European extraction.

In sum, the Muscovites arrived at the early modern game both late and short. They had to catch up to Europe, and they had to do it with few social resources. The only recourse was statism. The early reliance on state-initiated development had a profound impact on Russian history. Over the course of the next three centuries, while western European states elaborated republican government in response to emergent intellectual trends and class interests, Russia remained under the autocratic control of a tiny ruling class. The reason for this divergence cannot be that these stimuli were completely absent in Russia, for they were not. As concerns political ideas, the liberal political philosophies that republicans in Europe found so attractive were available and being discussed in Russia as early as the mid-eighteenth century. Catherine the Great's intense love of Montesquieu's ideas offers an excellent case in point. In the nineteenth century, Russian thinkers citing European political philosophy often openly attacked autocracy as unjust. The Westernizers are the most famous of them. As concerns new class interests, the Russian nobility was liberated from service in the mid-eighteenth century and emerged as a potential independent political class. In 1825 a small number of nobles (inspired, of course, by European political philosophy) attempted to overthrow autocracy. Later in the nineteenth century, populists and socialists, claiming to speak for the peasantry and the growing working class, took a similarly oppositional stance to the autocratic rule of the few. They launched what was perhaps the first modern political terror campaign, assassinating tsarist political officials indiscriminately. The spark, then, was present, but it never ignited a fire. Why not? Four obvious explanations present themselves.

First, the ruling elite—like all ruling elites—had no real interest in surrendering its authority to other groups. They were jealous of their power, plain and simple. Some commentators (Richard Pipes comes to mind) have criticized the Russian ruling class for its seemingly endless desire to maintain power. But to expect otherwise would be to deny the most basic element of human nature: selfishness. Moreover, the Russian elite usually had the power to enforce its virtual monopoly on authority due to the absence of organized political interests in society. In early Muscovite times, there were basically none outside the church. In Muscovite times proper, there emerged a warrior class (the boyars and gentry) and a merchant guild, but both were created by the state. In the Petrine and Catherinian ages, Russian society developed further, but neither the liberated nobility nor the growing urban classes expressed much interest in political power. Toward the end of the nineteenth century, modern politics of a sort emerged in Russia, but it was only after the state had permitted it to emerge in the wake of the Great Reforms and the Revolution of 1905. When the autocracy found politics inconvenient, as in the Duma period, it remained able to mute oppositional voices.

Second, the ruling elite could always legitimize its monopoly on political power and its hesitancy to embrace liberal reform with reference to the European threat. The elite might have discussed liberal reforms, and it might even have created actual democratic institutions (the Dumas). But when push came to shove, its fear of Western invasion and domination drove it back to the autocratic state and its unique mobilizational power. Many commentators, George Kennan the most famous and influential of them, have labeled the Russian fear of the West a kind of paranoia. In this popular view the Russian ruling class, suffering from a historically conditioned sense of inferiority, displaced its own insecurity on the West. For them, the Europeans were always coming, even though a neutral observer would think otherwise. Yet the paranoia theory hardly seems credible (and indeed, seems somewhat deluded itself) given the cold, hard historical facts of Russian-European relations. Since the initial Muscovite encounter with Europe, European armies have repeatedly invaded Russia. In the seventeenth century the Poles, Ottomans, and Swedes came; in the eighteenth century the Swedes, Austrians, and Ottomans; in the nineteenth century the French, British, and Ottomans. No nation on earth has faced such continuous and deadly military pressure. To be sure, the Russian elite and the nation it led often initiated military action, but more often it did not. Given this established pattern, it hardly seems unreasonable for Russian leaders to be concerned about political reforms that might weaken Russia's ability to defend against the next onslaught.

Yet there was an even more powerful third reason for the continuity of autocratic government: namely, the obvious utility of autocratically led modernization in the context of Western modernization and a weak Russian society. We have already seen that Russia began its ascent to power in a very unfortunate circumstance. The ruling class was both under the gun of superior European forces and in possession of a country that was politically inert, technically unsophisticated, economically impoverished, and, given the country's open borders, vulnerable to attack on almost all sides. Despite these disadvantages as compared with Europe, the remarkable Muscovite reform effort succeeded in saving Russia from extinction by pursuing a new path to early modernity. But this effort simultaneously made Russian society a crea-

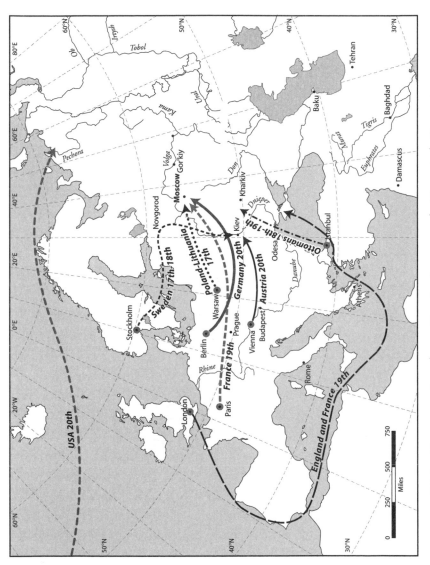

Major European Attacks on Russia, Seventeenth–Twentieth Centuries

ture of the state itself. There are two ways to look at this phenomenon. From a European perspective, the subordination of society to the state had all kinds of negative consequences: Autocratic organization stifled political action; the closed borders and tight control of the public sphere muted cultural and technical advance; state control of the economy fettered the efficiency of markets; and state-sponsored militarism promoted imperialism. From the viewpoint of the Russian elite, however, taking society under the state's wing had great advantages: Autocracy ensured unity of command and prevented wasteful political battles; cultural control promoted political stability and, with the proper investment, a focus of intellectual power on necessary projects; command economics ensured that while no one would get rich, no one (or almost no one) would starve, and that what most needed to be made would be made; and militarism enabled the state to put distance between itself and Europe, in addition to creating international prestige.

Both of these views are stilted, products of the confrontation between the European and Russian paths to modernity. But more than that, they are irrelevant because the Russian elite really had a very limited range of choices given Russia's geopolitical position and the nature of Russian society. The Europeans, it turned out, *were* always coming, and the Russian elite usually possessed few options — to protect itself and its nation — other than a recourse to state-initiated reform. Each episode of statist modernizing reform — under Peter I, Catherine II, Alexander I, Alexander II, Sergei Witte — served two functions. First, it reinforced the basic message that autocracy was the only effective mechanism for bringing Russia up to speed. Given the continued approach of the Europeans and the weakness of Russian society in the wake of the *last* reform effort, nothing else would work. Second, each state-sponsored reform fixed society in the form needed to fight the *last* war. In periods between conflicts, there was no powerful state stimulus, and thus society stagnated. When a new conflict appeared on the horizon, the Russian elite found its social resources obsolete. Obsolescence, of course, made the *next* state-sponsored reform effort all the more necessary.

Finally, it is clear that one of the primary anchors of autocracy and its program was that Russians identified with both in a deep, cultural sense. We would be fooling ourselves if, like the Marxists of old, we thought that the Russian ruling class was alone in believing in autocracy and its mechanisms. Far from it. Over the course of time, the affirmative defense of the Russian road to modernity formulated by ruling-class thinkers seeped down into the very cultural fabric of Russian society. We can see this in the popular doctrine of the Russian Tradition. It began to evolve in the seventeenth century, when the Muscovites first formulated the idea that they were defending something against Europe. We can see the seeds of the Russian Tradition, for example, in the Old Believers' visceral hatred of any foreign-inspired novelty. The doctrine itself, however, didn't come to flower until the later eighteenth century, the moment at which many Russian notables became acutely aware that they were sham Europeans. Suddenly a nativist urge sprang up in the Russian breast, and defense of the Russian Tradition became all the rage among conservatives. Prince Mikhail Shcherbatov's elegiac political philosophy, with its praise of Muscovite ways, illustrates this tendency. By the mid-nineteenth century, defense of the Russian Tradition had become both official doctrine ("Orthodoxy, Autocracy, and Nationality") and a kind of demipolitical movement (Slavophilism).

Historians have often described the Russian road to early modernity in terms of absences and failure. The Russians, they say, lacked a democratic impulse, a commitment to openness, a desire for free markets, and an interest in national self-determination. Therefore, the critics conclude, the Russians failed. But this is to interpret Russian history entirely from the European perspective. If we assume a more neutral stance, things look very different indeed. Russia did not really fail, rather the opposite. The country succeeded in staving off Europe for almost five centuries, whereas every other early modern polity collapsed. Russia accomplished this remarkable feat because of what it possessed (or rather built), not because of what it lacked. And what it possessed was, in the first instance, a highly effective, durable, and resourceful political system — autocracy. Relieved of the inefficiency of political infighting, autocratic power allowed the Russian ruling class to pursue an alternative path to early modernity, one characterized by a tightly controlled public sphere, a regulated command economy, and a state-engineered army. Using these means, the Russian elite was able to take a primitive, premodern state and transform it in the course of two centuries into one of the most powerful enterprises on earth. It is difficult to see how such a thing could be seen as a failure, at least until World War I.

7

From Early Modernity to Modernity

HISTORIANS, LIKE ALL SOCIAL SCIENTISTS, CLAIM not to take sides as they approach a topic. Most agree that a balanced or even neutral view is essential to accurate historical depiction. Yet the history of much of modern historical writing is one of bias. Historians often seem to be as unable to avoid partisanship as the common man. They take sides, often unknowingly, as a look at historical views of the Soviet Union suggests.

The Muscovite ruling class was blindsided by the sudden and unexpected appearance of aggressive early modern European states. Three centuries later, the successors of those Muscovite boyars were similarly surprised by the sudden appearance of aggressive *modern* European states. In the closing decades of the eighteenth century, British entrepreneurs discerned both the secrets of mechanical power and the mysteries of well-regulated free markets. We still don't know exactly why the industrial revolution happened when and where it did, but its geopolitical result is crystal clear — a massive increase in European military power followed by a new wave of crushing global imperialism. The slow and steady accumulation of European authority in the far corners of the world was supplanted by simple, sudden armed invasion. No traditional, early modern power, it seemed, could hope to withstand the assault of the Europeans with their rifles, machine guns, artillery, steamships, trains, and all the other fixtures of Victorian-era armed conquest.

Once again the Old World succumbed to the New, only this time the conquest was much more definitive. The Europeans, and the slaves they brought with them from Africa, settled the far reaches of the Americas. So too did they make southern Africa their home in large numbers; despots such as King Leopold of Belgium and Cecil Rhodes created virtual slave states in central Africa. European gunboats and the soldiers they carried subdued much of the southern rim of Eurasia — Palestine, Syria, Iraq, Iran, India, southeast Asia, and Australia. The Europeans even managed to force the Qing empire, every bit as advanced as any early modern Western state, into concessions that went well beyond the violation of sovereignty. The European message to the world was clear: Modernity was unstoppable, especially if it came bloody-minded and well armed.

The Russian ruling class of the early nineteenth century was slow to realize this basic truth. Like their Muscovite predecessors, they remained shielded by vast distances and protected by powerful autocratic government. The continued utility of both, even in the age of incipient industrialism, were admirably demonstrated in Napoleon's defeat and the subsequent Russian invasion of Europe. The psychological impact on the Russian ruling elite of Alexander I's victory cannot be overstated. With Russian troops in Paris, the elite must have thought there was no reason to worry about the humbled Europeans (and especially the pompous French). Hadn't the defeat of the Corsican demonstrated the preeminence of Russian civilization? Most of the Russian elite, thoroughly enamored with the superficialities of European life, refused to draw this troubling conclusion. Bolder souls — such as the Slavophiles — were more than willing to proclaim that the Russian way of life was at the very least *ethically* superior to the corruption they readily found festering in the European soul. It is perhaps true that these radical notions did not enjoy widespread popularity, but the more general notion that the Russian system was very sound could be heard in the highest echelons of authority. Witness, for example, the remarkably conservative habits of Nicholas I. Lost in his reactionary complacency, the tsar failed to see that his country was falling farther behind the West in terms of economic might and military capacity than ever before.

The sins of the father were, however, soon to be visited upon the son. In the early 1850s, the British and the French military establishments accomplished what would have been almost impossible before the industrial age: They shipped 60,000 troops hundreds of miles, maintained them (if not always in good order) for three years, and used them to defeat a huge Russian army *on Russian territory*. It is important to comprehend rightly what was being demonstrated in the Crimean War. The lesson was not, as we might instinctively believe, that European weapons were superior to those borne by the Russians. True, the Europeans were better armed than the Russians, but Nicholas's forces were suitably equipped according to the standards of the day. Rather, the Crimean debacle proved the preeminence of European logistics and the industrial system that supported them. The English and French showed that they could arm, transport, and deploy a huge army reasonably rapidly far from their shores; the Russians, alas, demonstrated they could *not* arm, transport and deploy a superior army several hundred miles from Moscow. Guns didn't turn the tide in the Crimea; the combination of coal, iron, and steam did. Russia was seen for what it was, a backward agricultural empire in the dawn of the industrial era.

As a result of this humiliating defeat, a good portion of the Russian ruling elite lost faith in the traditional Muscovite means of state-building. It is easy to see why. The very institution that the entire modernizing project had been built to produce — the army — had been defeated by shipborne Western forces on Russian soil just half a century after Napoleon's Grand Armée had been driven back to Paris. For many Russians this stunning capitulation seemed to confirm what Europhilic critics — the Westernizers — had been saying for some decades. Russia, they railed, was being held in check by autocracy and its concomitant institutions, and the country was therefore falling rapidly behind the liberalizing, industrializing West. The Russian Tradition, it appeared to many on what was soon to be called the Left, stood squarely in the way of historical progress. The old ways had made Russia early modern, but they could not make it modern.

And so Alexander II and, later, his grandson Nicholas II attempted to set Russia on a new course, one that was largely inspired by the European path to modernity. In the Great Reforms and the Witte-Stolypin periods, the authority of autocracy was augmented by new public bodies (the zemstvos, Duma, and the like), restrictions on public discourse were relaxed, the serfs were liberated and the economy liberalized, and the army was restructured (again) along European lines. Historians have long debated the efficacy of these alterations. Citing statistics suggesting that Russia was rapidly industrializing in the later nineteenth and early twentieth century, some scholars argue that Russia had successfully made the turn from the old Muscovite ways to the new European pattern. Russia, these optimistic historians believe, was on its way to becoming a modern European country. Others, pointing to the continued resistance of the autocratic government to liberalizing reforms, suggest that the elite was pouring new wine in old bottles. These pessimistic historians argue that Russia remained a backward place, incapable of European-style industrial modernization.

This question will never receive an answer, for Russian development (or lack of it) was halted by an unlikely historical conjuncture—the advent of World War I. Whether we believe Russia was progressing along the European road or not, the result of the Great War made one thing abundantly clear: Just as in the Crimean conflict, Russia was still behind the West in terms of its ability to generate and project military power. Imperial Germany, fighting a war on two fronts against much larger forces, managed to defeat the huge Russian armies in a matter of two years. Once again the Russian elite began to doubt autocracy. More important, the emergent Russian public began to doubt it as well. In the era of

Alexander I's reforms, the Russian public consisted of the upper nobility and the wealthy urban elite, both of whom were solidly wedded to the autocratic state and its reformist program. In Nicholas I's time, however, the public sphere had expanded in the wake of the liberalizing political reforms of the post-1905 settlement. In the war years, many elements (the nobility, urban classes, workers, soldiers, peasants, national minorities) espousing many different programs (monarchist, republican, socialist, agrarian) lost faith in autocracy and its institutional baggage. Given the disasters on the eastern front and the ensuing social crisis, we can hardly blame them.

Beset on all sides, the Old Regime crumbled. Shortly thereafter, the Bolsheviks came to power. To say that the rise of the Communists in Russia has been "extensively studied" would do violence to both the adverb and verb. More scholarly attention has been lavished on "1917 and all that" than any topic in human history. Its "extent" is perhaps best measured by the mania that inspired it. Moreover, many of those "studying" the Russian Revolution were really attacking or defending it in ways so obvious as to be pitiable. There is nothing sadder than the sight of partisans shabbily clothing their mystical politico-religious beliefs in the rags of "science." The entire enterprise represents a black day in modern historiography.

In point of fact, what happened in 1917 and how the Bolsheviks won out was reported rather accurately in the newspapers of the time. They tell a simple tale. In that fateful year there were only two factions struggling for power: educated urbanites who supported the liberal Provisional Government, which promised more European-style reforms, and impoverished city dwellers, soldiers, and peasants who wanted to take what they believed belonged to them from the rich. In the pitiful conditions of wartime Russia, the latter were much more numerous than the former, particularly on the streets of the swollen capital. Somewhat surprisingly, the mob of poor folk was also much better led than its sophisticated counterparts. The supporters of the Provisional Government were committed to the democratic process and therefore hamstrung by the niceties of parliamentary procedure and law. The leaders of the levelers — the Bolsheviks first among them — were committed to seizing power by any means necessary in the name of "the People." And so they did, in an almost bloodless coup in October 1917. The liberals were out, the millenarians were in.

Almost as much ink has been spilled regarding the Bolsheviks as on their victory in 1917. Indeed they are a confusing bunch. On one hand, they were themselves often the sons of the elite they swore to overthrow. Well-educated, highly articulate, and given to lofty theoretical abstraction, men such as Lenin were hardly brutes. On the other hand, they quickly demonstrated that they were capable of the most intense brutality in the name of the cause. Lenin himself rather casually ordered the summary execution of his enemies, suspected enemies, and even common folk to set an example to those who might think of becoming his enemies. It is little wonder that contemporary historians have been unable to reconcile the contradictions of what we might call the "two Lenins."

The reason for this inability to comprehend Lenin and his party as a single, sensible entity may be traced to the idea that the Bolsheviks were a political party in the democratic sense. Within the framework of nineteenth- and early-twentieth-century republics, political parties were basically groups of like-minded persons who provisionally banded together to pursue limited political goals. Clearly there was nothing provisional or limited about the Bolsheviks: Commitment to the party was total, and the goals were nothing short of mystical. Indeed the party of Lenin shared both of these characteristics with its closest modern sociological analogue—the radical religious cult. As we know from bitter experience, for the leaders and members of cults there is no contradiction between the loftiest ends and the crudest means. Martyring themselves or murdering others in pursuit of heaven is simply part of the divine plan. If they are not rewarded, then their descendants and indeed all mankind surely will be. Nothing must stand in the way of the rapture.

Their first order of business was to win the ongoing civil war against the Whites. In this struggle the Bolsheviks could give free reign to their well-intentioned barbarism without significant political risk. After all, they were fighting for the future of the Idea—this united the party—and their political program promised tangible benefits to the common person, which secured the support of the desperate, starving masses. The mindless savagery of the Whites was an unexpected bonus, as it alienated that part of the population that might have been sympathetic to the tsarist cause. The Bolsheviks, operating from the central industrial region of the country, destroyed the White armies in detail, one after another until there were no White armies left. The capitals of Europe filled with dispirited Russian émigrés, who, having lost the battle of the sword, took up the pen in the good fight.

The Bolsheviks, however, faced one last test before they

could declare complete victory. It was the most important test they ever faced. The proper course of action in the civil war was clear: The tsarist officers and those who fought beside them were the avowed foes of the Revolution and had to be annihilated. But what was a good Communist to do when armed opposition arose within the ranks of the party itself? Since the very inception of the movement, European socialists agreed that comrades were not to engage in physical combat. In principle, Marxism was an affair of the mind, not of the heart. Rational discussion would lead to the Truth, which had to be accepted by all according to the Leninist principle of "democratic centralism" (perhaps the first of the horrible blows dealt the Russian language by the Bolsheviks). But what would happen when the cadres refused to accept the Truth and wanted to continue the discussion?

Not surprisingly, this question arose in a very forceful way immediately after the civil war. The place was the Kronstadt naval fortress in the Gulf of Finland. There in 1921 a large group of hardened Revolutionary soldiers — all with excellent credentials — began to criticize democratic centralism as it was then practiced and proposed, inter alia, straightforwardly democratic reforms. What to do? Lenin ordered the Red Army to reduce the fortress and crush the counterrevolutionaries by whatever means necessary. This was accomplished at a horrible cost in human life. The Revolution — at least as Lenin understood it — had survived. But even more important, the Bolsheviks had learned three crucial lessons. First, Kronstadt demonstrated that socialists would put other socialists to the sword in the name of socialism, and even in very large numbers. The taboo against intraparty violence was broken once and for all. Second,

Kronstadt showed that terror worked as well within the party as without. Rational persuasion according to Marxist principles was all well and good, but a tangible threat of violence to those who stepped out of line was even better. Finally, Kronstadt proved that one could be a good international socialist even while murdering other socialists. Certainly other members of the European socialist movement were distressed by the need to put down the revolt, but they accepted that it was a need nonetheless. The Idea overrode other considerations in the minds of many Europeans, and besides, Russia was a brutal country.

Kronstadt handed the Bolsheviks the tools — violence, terror, and the blind trust of their Western comrades — they needed to build socialism. With the means then at their disposal, they began to consider a plan. It is important to recall that socialism at the time was nothing but an idea. Unlike capitalism, it did not exist in any natural state, nor had anyone ever tried to build it ex nihilo. The voluminous writings of Marx and Engels are embarrassingly silent on the practicalities of socialist construction. There was no road map to socialism.

There was, however, a road map to something that might be *called* socialism. Lenin himself was the first to realize this fact. He and his comrades were great admirers of Germany's wartime economy, in which the state assumed direct control over a good proportion of production and distribution. Whatever socialism might be, so the Bolsheviks must have thought, it was certainly about increased production and equitable distribution. The Germans had shown the way, but only through self-serving half measures taken in the interest of winning an imperialist war. Following what they believed were immutable laws of development, the Bolsheviks would push history forward by placing the state in direct control of *all* production and distribution. And they would call it socialism.

It was a good plan, but it had to wait. Upon the conclusion of the civil war the Bolsheviks found themselves in nearly the same predicament as Alexander II and his confederates in the wake of the Crimean conflict. They were a tiny elite in a huge, bankrupt country that had just been defeated by the more advanced powers of Europe. The catastrophes of the war and civil war had, in essence, returned Russia to a premodern state, at least in an infrastructural sense. Cultural institutions — schools, universities, scientific institutes — had crumbled. The industrial sector collapsed, and the economy again became almost entirely agrarian. The army consisted of poorly led and poorly armed conscripts who proved all too willing to turn on their masters for a crust of bread.

And so the party bided its time, giving itself a chance to prepare for the coming assault and giving society a moment to move past the worst of postwar poverty. The New Economic Policy (NEP) period achieved the latter but not the former. As the 1920s came to a close, the party remained something of an occupying force, despised by a good portion of the rural population. Moreover, the party bosses became convinced that war with the capitalist West was inevitable and even near. By the end of the decade, the waiting was over. Stalin's faction decreed that the only way to ensure long-term political stability (that is, Communist dictatorship) and gird the country against European invasion was to commence forthwith with the building of socialism. The lessons of Kronstadt were relearned: Once again, Communists shot Communists for Communism; terror surged through the ranks of the party; and foreign travelers turned a blind eye to or spoke condescendingly of the brutality of the Russian soul. It was a pathetic episode in the history of humanity.

Naturally the Bolsheviks proclaimed that the entire horrific campaign — collectivization, forced industrialization, the purging of class enemies — was pursued in the name of a creating the world's first socialist society. And so it was. But oddly enough, Soviet socialism turned out to bear a remarkable resemblance to the Russian tradition it pretended to transform. A tiny elite at the head of a slightly larger ruling class dominated the entire enterprise. There would be no politics in the ordinary republican sense. The engine of control was the state itself, operating with unrestricted license over the population. Subjects had no enforceable rights, but certain privileges would be granted and honored. The borders were closed and public discourse severely restricted. For those whose loyalty was proven, travel abroad was possible, as was access to foreign information. Land and labor were nationalized in the interest of the state. Subjects were granted use of the means of production (including their own bodies), but they did not directly own them. Finally, resources were poured into a military modernization program aimed directly at keeping the West at bay. In short, the Russians seem to have traveled the same road to modernity that they had traveled to early modernity, one characterized by autocracy, command economics, cultural insularity, and an emphasis on arms. To be sure, the ideologies that guided Muscovite and Soviet state-building were radically different, but the underlying interests, mechanisms, and results were remarkably similar, given the period separating them.

Today most historians are highly critical of the Bolshevik modernization program, and rightfully so, for it resulted in the unnatural deaths of millions of innocent Soviet citizens. The Communists — particularly under Stalin — were guilty of the gravest crimes against humanity. Their regime was illegitimate on those grounds alone. But still it must be understood that the Bolshevik program achieved its main goals and won the allegiance of most of the subject population. Using the traditional means of Russian state-building, the Bolsheviks managed to create the chief infrastructural characteristics of modernity as they were found in Europe and America. The Soviet Union, though ruled for much of its history by a ruthless dictatorship, was administered by a massive bureaucracy operating according to legislated rules. Every sector of Soviet life was governed by an office occupied by trained specialists. Though the public sphere was tightly controlled in the USSR, it was very large and well stocked. Soviet mass culture featured universal education, consumerism, and mass communications. The Soviet economy was nothing if not industrial. By the late Soviet period, most Russians worked in factories, and almost everything they consumed came out of those factories. Lastly, the Soviet military was at certain moments the most advanced in the world. Universal conscription, professional officers' colleges, and a commitment to military research and development made the Soviet armed forces second only to those of the United States. Not only did the Soviet program succeed within its borders, it provided much of the undeveloped world with a reproducible road to modern infrastructure. By the 1960s the Soviets were aiding dozens of nations in the Second and Third World along the Russian road.

During and after the Cold War, many Western commentators wondered how the Communists, after all their primitive brutality, remained in power for so long. The answer to this query is the same as the one offered for the question of the stability of the Muscovite and Imperial autocracies. The party had no interest in giving up power, and given the weakness of Russian society in the wake of Stalin's social-engineering campaigns, it faced no internal threat. The party, like the autocratic ruling class before it, was the only political element in the land. Further, as before, the elite could always excuse its power and policies with reference to the European threat. The fact that Europeans actually did invade Russia with horrendous results on two occasions in the twentieth century (discounting minor incursions), and that the Americans dedicated themselves to an undeclared war against Soviet Communism, only served to bolster this position. Moreover, statist modernization seemed to work well in the Russian context. In 1920 Russia was starving and defenseless; in 1960 Russia enjoyed a high standard of living and was a superpower. Finally, most Russians believed in Communism, particularly after it was Russianized in World War II. Certainly there was opposition. But we would be fooling ourselves if we did not believe that Russians identified with the Communist program, especially after the Great Patriotic War.

Given what they knew about their own history, there is no reason they should not have believed in Communism. The state had told them that pre-Soviet Russia was an oppressive, backward, poor, defenseless place. Though we can easily recognize this as self-aggrandizing propaganda, we can also see that from the perspective of the common Russian, this tale contained more than an element of truth. The most distant memories of most Soviet citizens of the postwar years were "Stolypin neckties," illiteracy, hunger, and defeat in 1905 and 1916. To be sure, Russians experienced unimaginably hard times in the 1920s, 1930s, and 1940s. But we have no reason to believe that most of them—those who did not run afoul of the Communist authorities—didn't imagine themselves as the builders of a new, more just, and modern society. Their sacrifice, so they may have thought, would be worth it in the end. And in the end, wasn't it? The country was modernized, the Germans were defeated, and by the 1960s Russians were better governed, educated, fed, and protected than anyone could remember. The Russian road to modernity, clothed in Communist guise, had delivered the goods for millions upon millions of Soviet citizens and their followers in the Second and Third Worlds.

8

The End of the Russian Moment

AT THE BEGINNING OF OUR EXPLORATION WE CRI-
tiqued the idea of beginnings, then began nonetheless. Now
we have occasion to repeat this hypocritical exercise with
reference to endings. But here our task is much easier. For
although Russian history goes on, a distinct period of it does
seem to have reached an obvious terminus in our lifetime. In
1991 the era of the Russian path to modernity ended, and a
new epoch in world history began.

The Russian road to modernity began in the sixteenth century, when a small group of primitive warriors set Russia on
the course to a new kind of society that was different from
yet as powerful as that developing in Europe. The Russian
road ended in 1991, when Russia suddenly and unexpect-
edly descended into a premodern condition. What happened
in between these dates may properly be called an epoch in
world history, one characterized by the struggle between

two competing paths to modernity, the European and the Russian. This was the Russian moment.

The history of the Russian moment constitutes a remarkable story. Its prehistory begins with the migration of the Slavs to the north and their encounter with the Rus'. Without either of these events, there would have been no Russian history, let alone a Russian moment in world history. The Rus' enterprise was poor, primitive, and beset on all sides. Had it not survived the onslaught of one or another Steppe peoples, Rus' history would have ended before the beginning of Russian history. But the Rus' lived on, even through Mongol domination. From there the scene shifts from Kiev to Moscow, where a new East Slavic state was built in an unforgiving northern environment. A fateful decision was then made: Russia turned toward Europe and was drawn into European affairs. Russian history might have ended then and there, for Russia — like the rest of the extra-European empires of the world — was not equipped to compete with the ascendant Europeans. Yet thanks to a lucky geopolitical position and a remarkable program of radical reforms, the Russians managed to develop a kind of state that, though without significant natural endowments, could withstand the European challenge. Here we find the deepest origins of the Russian moment, for the Muscovite state provided the key components to what would become the Russian road to early modernity and, later, modernity. Over the next two centuries the Russians employed these components — autocracy, control of the public sphere, command economics, and state-sponsored militarism — to fend off Europe and build a massive empire. Still, the Russian path was at this point more an evolved practice than a reproducible program for modernization. That changed with the arrival of the Bolsheviks, who codified the Russian road in Marxist terms and exported it to the developing world, again with considerable success. Russianesque states then appeared all over the globe — in China, Vietnam, and North Korea and throughout Eastern Europe.

And then the Russian moment in world history suddenly ended, at least in Russia. Why? Various explanations have been given for the shattering of the USSR and its system. The oldest and perhaps the most popular cites the administrative inefficiency of authoritarian governments and their cultural, economic, and military accoutrements. Communism, so the saying goes, just doesn't work. Another theory points to the putative moral failings of authoritarianism. Human nature, this account has it, is inherently freedom-loving and basically selfish. Any social system that does not take these facts into account functionally enslaves its inhabitants by limiting their natural rights. Both of these explanations go some distance in laying bare the underlying causes of the demise of the Russian road: The statist model proved unable to provide standards of living on a par with those found in the West, and it unduly limited the strivings of those people living under it. Of these things there can be no doubt.

But a more compelling and complete explanation can perhaps be rendered in terms of the weakening of the four buttresses of autocracy after the Second World War. The first hint that the ruling party elite might be willing to make concessions to society came in the era of Khrushchev. Having experienced the horror of Stalinism and the holocaust of the Great Patriotic War, the party basically cut a new deal with its members and society at large: There would be no more purges or social-engineering campaigns in pursuit of Communist modernity, though the myth of Communism would remain. The hypocrisy of pursuing private interests in a corrupt society while claiming to selflessly serve the public good ate away at the moral confidence of the party itself. By the 1980s even the elite had conceded that Communist Russia could not keep up with the West. The party lost faith in the Russian path and, bowing to popular pressure within and nationalist pressure without, began to relinquish power under the leadership of Gorbachev. He was able to carry through liberalizing reforms without a conservative backlash (or at least an effective one) because it was obvious that the Europeans were no longer coming with blood on their minds. Europe no longer threatened Russia, so there was no reason to maintain a form of organization that was built to defend Russia against European invasion. Finally, Russians began to forget what the Russian Tradition meant in the postwar years. Fifty years of hypocritical Communist ideology had taken its toll, as had increased contact with the West. Common Russians no longer felt that they were part of a great, progressive, civilizational project. They began to view Russian history somehow as a failure and the Russian Tradition (including or excluding Communism) as a pathology. They began to want, more than anything else, to be European.

Without its chief underpinnings, the Russian project rapidly collapsed in 1991. The party left power, never to return, and a new democratically minded elite took its place. The Warsaw Pact was dismantled, and new security arrangements were made with NATO. Russians quickly adopted Western attitudes, and millions left for the West. The basic structures of the Russian road to modernity all crumbled:

Autocracy was replaced by an evolving democracy; the tightly controlled public sphere was opened; the command economy was supplanted by a chaotic mix of banditry and capitalism; and the once mighty armed forces were scaled back. The Russian project had ended.

It is common today to look back on the Russian road to modernity as a fruitless exercise in oppression. According to this view, the Muscovites were despots, their Imperial successors were tyrants, and the Communists were bloodthirsty utopians. It would be ridiculous to deny that there is some truth in this interpretation, for Russian history is full of despots, tyrants, and utopians. But it is equally preposterous to forget the contribution of the Russian road to the well-being of millions and even billions of common people, both Russian and non-Russian. As a bearer of modernity, albeit not the best form, the Russian path represented a vast improvement over premodern life. Despite their suffering at the hands of countless selfish rulers, modern Russians and those who followed them generally lived better, longer, and more securely than their ancestors did. Recognizing this fact does not excuse or justify the brutality of statist modernization. Rather, it simply makes the Russian moment in world history comprehensible for the generations who will never know it.

9

Coda: What Might Have Been

✦

HISTORY, WE ARE OFTEN INFORMED, IS NOT A SCI-
ence. Unlike, say, physics, the study of the past does not
allow us to make predictions about the future, at least not
with very great accuracy. History does, however, offer explanations of past events. *This* happened, we commonly say,
because of X, Y, and Z. Some clever philosophers have argued that explanation is really retrospective prediction. That
is, if we had known about X, Y, and Z, then we would have
been able to predict their outcome. As seductive as this logic
is, it is not quite correct. Every historical explanation is at
once incomplete (we can't discover all the causal factors)
and speculative (we can't travel back through the years to
investigate). Historical causality is diffuse, and the past is
over.

Yet the philosophers' insight does help us clarify the nature of any historical explanation. When we say, "This happened because of X, Y, and Z," we are in fact suggesting
that *had it not been* for X, Y, or Z (or all of them in combination), then "this" would probably not have happened;

rather, something else would have happened. Historians are generally very hesitant to identify just what would have transpired in such cases (counterfactuals). This hesitancy has a rather baleful consequence: It leads people to believe that things had to turn out as they did. As we'll presently see, the case of Russia demonstrates that there were many other possibilities besides the one that came to pass.

Let us imagine that the Slavs did not migrate from the Danube basin to the east and north in the second half of the first millennium. There is reason to believe that they might have chosen not to move. What we now call Eastern Europe is a more hospitable environment than the areas that became northern Rus': Its seasons are milder, its soil is generally better, it is further from the Steppe (and the hostile pastoral nomads), and it is closer to the major trade routes of western Eurasia. So what would likely have happened if the Slavs had stayed in the region roughly between the Elbe and Dnieper? There certainly would have been no Russian history as we presently understand it, for there would have been no Russia, at least in the Muscovite heartland of the Oka-Moskva mesopotamia. That hostile region would have probably been colonized by other agriculturalists, perhaps the German-speaking peoples who found their way to the Baltic littoral, or even Swedes. In contrast to the actual Slavic settlement of the north, both of these colonization efforts would have been conducted under the authority of an established European kingdom (the German Empire or the Swedish crown, respectively). Having successfully invested this vast area, we can easily imagine that one of these two states would have wielded tremendous power in the early modern and modern periods — just as Russia did.

The Slavs, of course, migrated. But what if the Vikings had not traveled to Rus' and set up shop? Again, there were a variety of reasons to avoid the east. In contrast to Normandy, Britain, and Sicily, northeastern Eurasia was not terribly attractive terrain. None of the amenities of post-Roman civilization were available in this cold, rustic region, not that the Vikings were very cultivated themselves. There was some international trade, which was always a plus from the Viking point of view. Yet there wasn't very much of it — Arab silver, slaves, amber, furs, some rough forest products, but that was about it. So what would Russian history be without the Rus'? It would not have been "Russian," that much is certain. Though the East Slavic region was comparatively poor, it would have nonetheless probably attracted other conquerors. There were a number of imperial candidates: Bulgars, Khazars, and any number of different peoples of the Great Steppe. Or perhaps one of the Slavic tribes would have risen to dominance. After conquest or self-organization, the Slavic story becomes manifestly more difficult to forecast. As all of these probable conquerors (save the Slavs themselves) had a more eastern orientation than the Rus', perhaps the East Slavs would have remained in the orbit of central Eurasia rather than drifting toward Europe via contact with Byzantium, much like Transoxiana.

In the event, the Vikings came and subdued the Dnieper basin and northern territories. And so, as we know, did the Mongols. But we also know that they almost decided not to conquer Rus'. The Mongols' first incursion was in 1223. On that occasion they defeated a Rus' army on the Kalka River. Then they vanished as quickly as they appeared. More than a decade later, of course, they returned. But what if they hadn't? What difference would it have made? The answer depends on our feelings concerning the impact of the Mongol assault. Some scholars have argued that Russian development was stunted by the Mongols. Under this scenario, Russia sans Mongols would have enjoyed (if that is the right word) a history like other "European" states. We've already pointed out considerable difficulties with this interpretation, so there is no need to rehearse them again here. A more reasonable gloss is that Russia sans Mongols would have been Russia sans its Muscovite core. In light of the fact that each of the major ethnic groups of western Eurasia eventually united under one crown, there is no reason to believe that the East Slavs would not have done the same. Not, however, under Moscow, for the Muscovites were creatures of the Mongols and owed their political success to them, at least in large measure. In short, the Mongols made Muscovy possible, so we have to venture that without the Mongols, there would have been no Muscovy.

The Mongols came, and the Muscovites rose to prominence. But what if the Mongols had chosen another client to use as order keeper and tax collector? We know that, in fact, the Mongols did not place all their bets on the Muscovites. On more than one occasion Sarai advanced the ruler of Suzdal' or Tver to the grand princely throne. What if the Kipchaks had favored one of these houses as they favored the Muscovite line? Would the course of events have been materially different? It is very hard to say, as we do not know very much about the internal organization of most

Rus' principalities in the northeast. Were they more democratic than the Muscovite realm? Were they more autocratic? Interesting questions, but, given the limitations of the
sources, we will probably never be able to offer any satisfying answers to them. Yet it seems probable that the Muscovite line was distinguished from its Rurikid competitors in
at least one principal way: The successors of Danil of Moscow were unusually talented men. In the thirteenth, fourteenth, and fifteenth centuries it was their skill, rather than
any political system, that seems to have been crucial for
Muscovite success. Unless one of the other Rurikid branches
were able to produce a similar string of remarkably capable
leaders — an improbable event, to be sure — it seems unlikely
that Russia would have risen as fast and as far as it did, or
that the country would have been able to mount an effective
defense against European aggression.

Russia rose under Muscovite leadership, and it kept the
Europeans at bay. But what, we might well ask, would have
transpired if this military effort had been unnecessary? What
if the Europeans had not created a new kind of imperial
state capable of projecting its power all over the globe? As
we've said, historians have invested tremendous effort in at-
tempting to discover how the "European Miracle" occurred,
and they have reached no consensus. Ming and Qing China
were every bit as economically, technically, and (until the
deployment of gunpowder armies by the Europeans) militarily capable as the various states of western Eurasia. This
is to say that we could as easily be scratching our heads over
the "Chinese Miracle" as the "European Miracle." Had Europe remained a traditional premodern *Kulturraum*, Russia's
history surely would have been very different. Without the

need to defend themselves against advanced, predatory European powers, the Muscovites would have had no reason to implement the series of reforms — creating a powerful central government, closing the borders, nationalizing resources, forging a huge military establishment and empire — that came to characterize the Russian autocratic tradition for centuries to come. Russia would have remained, like Europe, a cookie-cutter premodern empire, just like all the ones that had existed in Eurasia over the past three millennia. Of course, supposing the Chinese initiated the same imperial program as the Europeans, then it seems probable that Russia would have found itself on the very edge of the European subdivision of the Chinese dominated world system — a bit like Tibet after the age of European supremacy along the China Sea coast. Assuming (and here we enter the realm of pure speculation) the Europeans succeeded in ousting the Chinese, the Russians would have been brought into the European sphere as a primitive, poor sister. Again, the example of modern Tibet presents itself.

But Europe rose, the Muscovite ruling class responded, autocracy was built, Russia modernized *à la Russe*, the Europeans were fended off, and the country remained independent. At several moments, however, it seemed as if the game was up: during the Time of Troubles, the Napoleonic invasions, World War I, and World War II. On each of these momentous occasions, European forces penetrated deeply into the Russian heartland, destroyed the Russian army, and took or nearly took Moscow. What if the invaders had succeed in consolidating their power in Russia? In each instance, Russia's history would certainly have been different, but in different ways.

In the early modern period, Europeans engaged in extensive imperialism in western Eurasia, but never very successfully if judged by modern standards. With comparatively few exceptions, the major states and their titular ethnic populations remained where they were throughout the era: the Spanish in Spain, the French in France, the English in England, the Germans in the German Empire, and so on. The Muslims might be expelled, the Jews run out of town, the Huguenots exiled, or the Scots sent to Ireland, but by and large transfer of huge populations within Europe — ethnic cleansing, forced relocation, colonization — was not considered a reasonable option at the end of even the most successful military campaign.

Thus we can say with some assurance that even if the Poles or the French were to have hung on to Moscow after their respective conquests, the result would not have been Polish or French colonization. Rather the Poles and French would have imposed a new royal line — probably of Polish or French origin — on the Russian ruling class. From the early modern perspective, there was nothing unusual in such an arrangement: Kings were replaceable and were indeed often replaced, usually by foreigners (if the word has any meaning in this context). The Rurikid themselves claimed to be foreigners. Further, many of the boyar clans traced their ancestry (fictively) to places as far away as Rome, so it is doubtful that they would have objected to the right candidate. In fact, we know they didn't: The boyars agreed to accept a Polish ruler during the Time of Troubles (though their plan came to naught), and in the eighteenth century their successors embraced a series of Germans, the most notable of whom was Catherine the Great. Thus it seems safe to say that had the Poles or French conquered Russia permanently, the course of Russian history would have been altered only slightly. By the mid-sixteenth century, Muscovy was already a formidable state featuring a stable ruling class, a functional political system, and a vague sense of national identity. In other words, to statesmen of the era Russia seemed to be a permanent fixture on the western Eurasian political map. It could be ruled, but not eliminated.

This attitude changed dramatically in the early twentieth century. With the advent of rabid nationalism, populist statesmen — kings, ministers, and politicians alike — began to find it politically advantageous to shout about a nation's right to territories within western Eurasia itself. The staid classical order in which the major states were fixed, political and ethnic bounderies were allowed to differ, and the notion of colonizing within Europe was anathema was at an end. The imperceptible evolution toward intra-European colonization began, perhaps, with the unification of Germany and Italy at midcentury. "Unification" is itself a tendentious misnomer — it would be more proper to speak of the "creation" of Germany and Italy, two entities that had never before existed. Soon it became au courant to speak of "Greater" this and "Greater" that, as if no European state was satisfied with its existing borders. Matters came to a head in World War I, when every combatant save the United States openly fought to alter the political and ethnic landscape.

It was, then, in the course of the First World War that Russia first seriously risked being dismantled. In fact, the Russian Empire was dismantled in part under the Treaty of Brest-Litovsk, though the Muscovite core and Siberia remained in Bolshevik hands. It was only the capitulation of the Germans to the Western Allies that brought Eastern Ukraine back into the fold. Yet even if the Germans had triumphed and succeeded in enforcing the dictates of Brest-Litovsk, expulsion of the natives and outright German colonization could not have been expected. Germany would have grown, Ukraine might have emerged as its client state, and Bolshevik Russia would have proceeded according to its own internal dynamics toward the disaster of state socialism.

Obviously, the Second World War presents us with an entirely more severe type of intra-European imperialism. A few nationalists (the Russian thinker Danilevskii, for instance) dreamed of colonizing parts of Europe; Hitler actually set himself and the entire German people to the hateful task. His object was no less than the enslavement of the Slavs to the expanding German "master race." Poland, Belarus, Ukraine, and Russia were to become German *Lebensraum*. It is frightening to recall how close this racist lunatic came to achieving his aim, for the consequences would have been disastrous for the entire globe but particularly for the Slavs and Germans. The former would have suffered the yoke of German servitude, a yoke whose weight was such that it would have killed tens of millions in time. One thing is absolutely certain: Russia would have ceased to be Communist, for the Nazis would have murdered summarily the bulk of the Bolshevik hierarchy. But as fate would have it, German rule would probably have been relatively brief, for it seems unlikely the United States — having already embarked on a murderous terror campaign against German cities — would have hesitated for a moment to use atomic weapons against the Nazis. What would postwar Russia have been like if the Nazis had been defeated in this way? It is painful to imagine. As it was, the suffering of the Soviet peoples defies conventional description.

We have gotten a bit ahead of ourselves. Let us return in time to investigate hypothetical scenarios in which one or another internal reform effort, instead of failing, succeeded. As we have seen, three such state-sponsored campaigns did, in fact, make a lasting impact on Russia: that which created autocracy in the later fifteenth and early sixteenth centuries, the Petrine reforms of the early eighteenth century, and the Bolshevik program in the 1920s and 1930s. All were basically of the same character, and all led to a dramatic increase in state power over society and modernization *à la Russe*. The principal failures also number three: Catherine's Enlightenment-inspired initiative in the later eighteenth century, the Great Reforms of the second half of the nineteenth century, and Gorbachev's perestroika. Let us take each in turn.

Catherine's object was to moderate the authority of autocracy by introducing "intermediary bodies," an idea she cribbed directly out the pages of Montesquieu's *Spirit of the Laws*. Had she succeeded in this, it is not hard to imagine Russia evolving into something like a sort of *Ständestaat*. This result would not have been of the general European variety (if there is a general European variety), but whatever it was would have probably been much more open to the liberalizing movements of the nineteenth century than the regimes that actually appeared after Catherine. In this scenario, however unlikely, Russia might well have joined the other great powers of western Eurasia in the reasonably peaceful march toward republican government and industrial capitalism. Venturing any further would be pure, unfounded speculation. In the event, Catherine's reform was cut short by half-measures, the recalcitrance of the serf-owning ruling class, and ultimately the cautionary tale of the French monarchy. Catherine loved the philosophes, that is, until their followers murdered Louis XVI in a fit of revolutionary zeal. There is reform and there is *reform*.

Alexander II found himself in much deeper water and was therefore more committed to change than was his enlightened German predecessor. His object was to make autocracy more inclusive and set Russia on a European economic road. There are those who argue that he succeeded in both these initiatives. At the end of the century the Russian government was, after a manner, pluralistic, and the economy was industrializing, albeit under the hand of the state. The road was rocky, as the experience of 1905 demonstrated, but even the inept Nicholas II managed to stay his grandfather's reformist course for a time. Had Russia's progress not been halted by World War I, or had the Russians triumphed in that conflict, things would have been very different indeed. Most obviously, the Bolsheviks would never have come to power, despite the supposedly inexorable workings of class struggle. With the radical socialist threat out of the way, it is not difficult to picture Russia continuing its evolution toward liberalism in the political and economic spheres. The monarchy might not have survived the transition, but Russians in general still would likely be much better off today had a certain Serbian nationalist not shot a certain Austrian archduke.

Our final example of reform gone wrong is of much more recent vintage. Like its predecessors, it appeared in the only way large-scale reforms can appear in an autocracy — at the initiative of a far-sighted, charismatic ruler. Our hero is of course Mikhail Gorbachev. His goal was superficially different than those of Catherine and Alexander II, both of whom were enamored of Western models. Gorbachev, just like Lenin before him, had no clear model: He was still building socialism, and the kind of thing he had in mind was nowhere to be found in the annals of human history. It is a testament, perhaps, to the inherent limits of the imagination that he hit upon a program that Alexander II would have recognized: He was going to pluralize the government and free the serfs, so to say. Had he succeeded — and he might well have, for the collapse of the Soviet Union was nothing if not a contingent event — the history of the late twentieth century would have traveled a somewhat different road than it did in actuality. The Soviet Union would have at the very least decentralized, if not dissolved entirely. Russia would doubtless have multiparty politics, the sine qua non for all modern, legitimate states. The economy would have suffered a momentary collapse, but the catastrophes of the early 1990s might have been avoided. The Cold War might well have ended as the Communist Party slipped from power and its "anti-imperialist" program became a dim memory. In short, Russia would have become socialist in the way all European governments are socialist — in name only. As it happened, the pent-up desire of seventy-odd years of totalitarian and semitotalitarian rule made the political elite and the people it ruled impatient for freedom. Gorbachev's evolutionary approach was overtaken by events. The government was, in the end, haphazardly pluralized, to an extent that stable multiparty politics became impossible and a return to the "strong hand" more likely. And the serfs were freed willy-nilly, though they remained landless (metaphorically speaking) and therefore impoverished, just as was the case under Alexander II.

There was, then, nothing inevitable about the formation, progress, and end of the Russian moment in world history. Things could have been different, as we have seen. That they were not is the result of myriad historical accidents, now lost in the fog of time. Yet it would be a mistake to regard the Russian moment itself as nothing but the product of blind chance, for it was not. As I hope has become clear in the course of this presentation, there was a kind of gravitational force that constantly pulled Russia in the direction of autocracy and repeatedly overcame forces that might have caused her to abandon it. That force was the self-interest of the Russian ruling class.

From the moment the autocratic system was constructed in the sixteenth century, the ruling class became solidly wedded to it. The reason is rather simple: Autocracy enabled the elite to successfully defend its interests both against external threats (Europe) and internal threats (its subjects). Having skillfully constructed this remarkable instrument of rule, and having seen its utility repeatedly demonstrated in many spheres, the Russian ruling class *reasonably* refused to abandon it for a very long period. The anchor of the Russian moment in world history, the element that fostered Russia's historical continuity, was the tenacity of the ruling class in maintaining autocracy.

This being so, the only way to destroy autocracy in Russia was to sever the ruling class from it. The historical record contains two kinds of scenarios in which such a divorce seemed possible — invasion by foreigners and a loss of political resolve by the elite itself. Had the Poles, Swedes, French, or Germans succeeded in invading and holding Russia, the ruling class might have been removed from power and autocracy dismantled. That this did not happen was the result of the ruling class's skill, determination, and a good measure of simple luck. Similarly, had Catherine, Alexander, or Gorbachev managed to convince the ruling few that there was another way to maintain power and defend Russia against its enemies, the elite might have given up on the Russian *Sonderweg*. Again, that this did not transpire is the result of many factors, among them chance. In the end, it was the second scenario that brought down autocracy in Russia after its four-hundred-year run. The Russian ruling class lost faith in the system that had served it so long and so well. It was abandoned, at least momentarily, and the entire order collapsed. Russia is now, for the first time in half a millennium, experimenting with a radically new way of doing things. Whether it will succeed in the new or return to the old, only time will tell.

CHRONOLOGY

6th century	Slavs appear in the historical record north of the Danube.
6th–9th century	Slavs migrate north and east, opening new regions to agriculture and driving back Uralic hunter-gatherers.
9th century	A band of Vikings, the Rus', arrives in the Dnieper region, asserting dominion over the Slavs and taking over international trade. The Rus' raid Byzantine territories.
10th century	The Rus' and Slavs convert to Orthodox Christianity. The Khazars of the lower Volga are defeated.
11th century	Kievan Rus' becomes a major regional power with limited contacts in Europe, the Middle East, and Central Asia.

12th century	The empire begins to fragment into many minor Rurikid principalities. War breaks out with the Polovtsy.
13th century	The Mongols conquer Rus'. Moscow emerges as one of the main Rus' principalities.
14th century	The Metropolitan of Kiev relocates to Moscow, signaling a shift of political power to the northeast. The Tatars are defeated at Kulikovo Field but burn Moscow to the ground two years later. Tamerlane conquers the Golden Horde.
15th century	The Golden Horde collapses and regional Tatar khanates appear. The Ottomans capture Constantinople. Ivan III marries Sophia Paleologa. European diplomats visit Moscow for the first time.
16th century	Ivan IV crowned "tsar." He introduces the first gunpowder infantry force. European technicians are recruited. The khanates of Kazan' and Astrakhan' are taken. Muscovite forces are bloodied in the Livonian War. The Rurikid dynasty ends with the death of Tsar Feodor.

Early 17th century   The Time of Troubles takes place. Moscow is occupied by the Poles, then liberated by a national militia. Mikhail Romanov is chosen as tsar.

Mid–17th century   Serfdom is imposed. Foreign mercenaries are recruited to fight the Poles, Lithuanians, and Swedes. The Russian Orthodox Church suffers a schism. Muscovite forces take left-bank Ukraine.

Late 17th century   Muscovite armies fail to occupy the Great Steppe. A treaty is signed with the Qing establishing the Russian border with China.

Early 18th century   Peter the Great launches his Europeanizing reforms. Saint Petersburg becomes the capital of the empire. Russia defeats Sweden in the Great Northern War. The Russian Academy of Sciences is founded.

Mid–18th century   Moscow University is founded. The gentry is liberated from mandatory state service.

Late 18th century   Catherine the Great initiates more Europeanizing reforms. Russian forces drive into the Great Steppe, Lithuania, and Poland.

Early 19th century   Russian forces take the northern Caucasus. Napoleon invades Russia and takes Moscow but is driven out. Russian forces arrive in Paris.

Mid–19th century   A rebellion by reformist officers (the Decembrists) is put down. The conservative doctrine "Orthodoxy, Autocracy, and Nationality" is promulgated. Slavophilism appears. Russia is defeated in the Crimean War. The Great Reforms are undertaken, including the emancipation of the serfs. Russian forces occupy Central Asia.

Late 19th century   Radicals begin a terror campaign against autocracy. Alexander II is assassinated. Industrialization begins, with government sponsorship.

Early 20th century   Russia is defeated by Japan in the Far East. The Revolution of 1905 sets the government on a reformist path. Political parties form. Stolypin undertakes further land reform. Russia is defeated and invaded in the First World War. The Romanov dynasty ends. The Bolsheviks overthrow the Provisional Government.

Mid–20th century   Stalin begins forced collectivization of agriculture, forced industrialization, and the elimination of "class enemies." The Soviet Union rapidly modernizes. The Nazis invade the Soviet Union and inflict horrible losses but are repulsed.

Late 20th century   Khrushchev brokers a new deal with the Communist Party and society. The era of massive social engineering ends. Standards of living improve, though not at the Western pace. The party, under Gorbachev, launches reforms. The Soviet Union collapses and fifteen independent republics emerge.

BIBLIOGRAPHIC NOTE

THE LITERATURE ON RUSSIAN HISTORY, EVEN IN English, is vast. The present bibliographic essay is intended to provide the reader with only a few basic texts that touch on the issues presented in this book.

Though there are many general interpretations of Russian history, most are not worth reading. Three exceptions are Richard Pipes, *Russia under the Old Regime* (New York: Scribner, 1974); Richard Hellie, "The Structure of Modern Russian History: Towards a Dynamic Model," *Russian History/Histoire Russe* 4 (1977), 1–22; and Edward Keenan, "Muscovite Political Folkways," *Russian Review* 45 (1986), 115–81. These works are provocative yet very well informed. Indeed, much of what is found in this book was inspired by them.

A good book on the early history of Eurasia is David Christian's *A History of Russia, Central Asia, and Mongolia*, vol. 1: *Inner Eurasia from Pre-History to the Mongol*

Empire (Oxford and Malden, Mass.: Blackwell Publishers, 1998). The most interesting work on the origins and migrations of the Slavs (and everyone else, for that matter) is currently being done by population biologists. Luigi Cavalii Sforza's *Genes, Peoples and Languages* (Berkeley: University of California Press, 2000) provides an intelligible description of the science involved, as well as an overview of its findings to date. For more detailed accounts focusing on the Slavs and their neighbors, see Vladimir Orekhov et al., "Mitochondrial DNA Sequence Diversity in Russians," *Federation of European Biochemical Societies Letters* 445 (1999), 197–201; and Spencer R. Wells et al., "The Eurasian Heartland: A Continental Perspective on Y-Chromosome Diversity," *Proceedings of the National Academy of Sciences* 98 (2001), 10244–49. For a recent analysis of the linguistic and archeological evidence, see P. M. Barford, *The Early Slavs: Culture and Society in Early Medieval Eastern Europe* (Ithaca, N.Y.: Cornell University Press, 2001). The most readable single-volume introduction to the formation and early history of the Rus' empire is surely Simon Franklin and Jonathan Shepard's *The Emergence of Rus', 750–1200* (London and New York: Longman, 1996). All the relevant literature is cited there.

The history of the Mongol-Rus' interaction is nicely summarized and analyzed in Charles Halperin, *Russia and the Golden Horde: The Mongol Impact on Russian History* (Bloomington: Ind.: Indiana University Press, 1985). A revisionist approach, stressing the importance of the Mongols on early Rus' and Muscovite history, is found in Donald G. Ostrowski, *Muscovy and the Mongols: Cross-Cultural Influences on the Steppe Frontier, 1304–1589* (Cambridge and

New York: Cambridge University Press, 1998). The rise and early history of Muscovy is ably treated in Robert Crummey, *The Formation of Muscovy, 1304–1613* (London and New York: Longman, 1987). The best book on the Muscovite reaction to the challenge of Europe in any language is doubtless Richard Hellie's seminal *Enserfment and Military Change in Muscovy* (Chicago: University of Chicago Press, 1971).

The dramatic changes of the Petrine epoch are nicely presented in Lindsey Hughes's encyclopedic *Russia in the Age of Peter the Great* (New Haven, Conn.: Yale University Press, 1998). For a more biographical view of Peter, see Paul Bushkovitch, *Peter the Great: The Struggle for Power, 1671–1725* (Cambridge and New York: Cambridge University Press, 2001). Catherine the Great's tumultuous era and her abortive attempt at reform are vividly portrayed in Isabel de Madariaga, *Russia in the Age of Catherine the Great* (New Haven, Conn.: Yale University Press, 1981). The following period, which featured further attempts at altering Russia's path, is described in David Saunders, *Russia in the Age of Reaction and Reform, 1801–1881* (London and New York: Longman, 1992), and Hans Rogger, *Russia in the Age of Modernization and Revolution, 1881–1917* (London and New York: Longman, 1983). For those interested in the course of Russian imperial expansion from Muscovite times to the fall of the Romanov regime, one can do no better than John LeDonne's *The Russian Empire and the World, 1700–1917: The Geopolitics of Expansion and Containment* (New York: Oxford University Press).

More has been written on the Bolshevik seizure of power than on any other subject in Russian history. This topic is also among the most divisive among the experts. For a conservative perspective, stressing the ruthlessness of the Bolsheviks, see Richard Pipes, *The Russian Revolution, 1899–1919* (New York: Alfred A. Knopf, 1990). For a liberal view, stressing popular support for the Bolsheviks, see Diane P. Koenker and William Rosenberg, *Strikes and Revolution in Russia, 1917* (Princeton, N.J.: Princeton University Press, 1989). A neutral survey is John Thompson, *Revolutionary Russia, 1917* (New York: Macmillan, 1989).

The literature on the Stalinist period is large and growing by the day. A traditional though still serviceable view emphasizing the brutality of the Stalinist dictatorship is Roy Medvedev, *Let History Judge: The Origins and Consequences of Stalinism*, rev. and exp., edited and translated by George Shriver (Oxford: Oxford University Press, 1989). A more focused treatment that gives due attention to the modernity (as well as brutality) of the Stalinist project is Stephen Kotkin's *Magnetic Mountain: Stalinism as a Civilization* (Berkeley: University of California Press, 1995).

Many books have already been written purporting to explain why the Soviet Union collapsed. For a summary and examination of opinions, see David Rowley, "Interpretations of the End of the Soviet Union: Three Paradigms," *Kritika: Explorations in Russian and Eurasian History* 2: 2 (2001), 395–426.

The most incisive interpretation of the entire Soviet experience is Martin Malia's *The Soviet Tragedy: A History of Socialism in Russia, 1917–1991* (New York: Free Press, 1994). On the world-historical significance of the collapse of Soviet Communism, see Francis Fukuyama, *The End of History and the Last Man* (New York: Free Press, 1992).

INDEX

✛